Psychology for Kids II

40 Fun Experiments That Help You Learn About Others

JONNI KINCHER

Edited by Pamela Espeland

free spirit PUBLISHING®
Works for kids™

Library of Congress Cataloging-in-Publication Data

Kincher, Jonni, 1949–

Psychology for kids II : 40 fun experiments that help you learn about others / Jonni Kincher ; edited by Pamela Espeland.

p. cm.

Includes bibliographical references and index.

ISBN 0-915793-83-0

1. Psychology—Experiments—Juvenile literature. 2. Psychology, Experimental—Juvenile literature. [1. Psychology—Experiments. 2. Personality tests. 3. Experiments.] I. Espeland, Pamela, 1951– . II. Title. III. Title: Psychology for kids two. IV. Title: Psychology for kids 2.

BF198.7.K56 1995

155.2'8—dc20 94-46251

CIP

AC

10 9 8 7 6

Printed in the United States of America

Cover and book design by MacLean & Tuminelly
Cover illustration by Nathan Jarvis
Text illustrations by Nathan Jarvis and Lisa Wagner
Index compiled by Theresa Wolner and Eileen Quam

Free Spirit Publishing Inc.
400 First Avenue North, Suite 616
Minneapolis, MN 55401
(612) 338-2068
help4kids@freespirit.com
www.freespirit.com

Dedication

To my parents, Jim and Clara Reay

To my father for answering most of my questions about the universe,
and to my mother for always being an exemplary role model for problem-solving.

If you have someone to answer many of your questions
and someone else to show you how to figure out the things that don't exactly have an answer,
you have everything you need to experiment and explore the universe.

Acknowledgments

I have never known anyone to be so generous with his or her time as Jim Matiya. I am more than grateful for all of the resources, input, and insights he shared to help this book come into being. There is no amount of "thanks" that would be adequate!

I also greatly appreciate those who contributed experiments: Stacy Dunn, Amy Geyer, Malia C. Novak, and Lisa L. Rybak. Adam Kincher proved to be an able research assistant, and as always I am grateful. Felicia Ann Palumbo and Ava Touloupakis helped by trying out an experiment—thanks!

As before, thanks to Judy Galbraith and Pamela Espeland and all the others at Free Spirit whose names and duties may not be known to me, but who do what they do with the pride and professionalism of true artists.

CONTENTS

LIST OF REPRODUCIBLE PAGES

Foreword

Jonni Kincher's original *Psychology for Kids* makes it fun, exciting, and challenging to learn about yourself. *Psychology for Kids II* draws upon your natural curiosity so you can learn about your friends, classmates, family members, and others. In this wonderful book, you'll find 40 different experiments designed to help you discover other people's beliefs and attitudes, perceptions, differences, styles of learning, and much more. Open it anywhere, jump into psychology, and you'll see how enjoyable and inspiring it can be.

Each experiment in this book is meant to be fun *and* educational. Each communicates Jonni Kincher's personal commitment to and love of psychology and learning.

Have you ever wondered what other people are thinking, perceiving, and believing? Have you ever asked yourself, "Why do people act the way they do?" *Psychology for Kids II* doesn't give you the answers. Instead, it helps you find answers for yourself. With this book and your own spirit of adventure, you'll uncover answers to questions about one of the most interesting subjects on earth: the psychology of being human.

Have fun!

Jim Matiya
Instructor of Psychology, Carl Sandburg High School, Orland Park, IL
Editor, *Psychology: Special Interest Group of the National Council for the Social Studies Newsletter*

Introduction

Life is like a gigantic, challenging puzzle—a maze with twisting paths, changing goals, surprising obstacles, and dead ends. Psychology is a tool that can help you find your way through the maze.

If you didn't already enjoy challenges, then games and puzzles would be work for you instead of play. You wouldn't get such a thrill from solving a problem or from turning confusion into order. I'm guessing that you do enjoy challenges, and that's part of why you're reading this book. You like to learn. You want to know and understand many things. If nature had not made us—and you—so curious, we never would have explored other lands or invented new tools. There would be no need for psychology.

One of the things we most want to know about is ourselves. My first *Psychology for Kids* book helps young people to learn more about themselves through 40 self-tests called Personal Style Inventories, or PSI's. Maybe you've already taken the self-tests in *Psychology for Kids.* If you haven't, you might want to try.

We also want to know about other people. *Psychology for Kids II* helps you to learn more about other people through 40 informal experiments and experiences. They are based in science, but they feel like games.

Almost as important as what you will learn in this book is the way you will learn it: by trying things firsthand and seeing for yourself what happens. Have fun with these experiments. Do a few, do a lot, skip around, and repeat the ones you like best. You may even want to create experiments of your own.

Almost every experiment can be done with pencil and paper. For some, you may need a few common objects, like a ball or toothpicks, but these aren't hard to find. You may have to make a few trips to the photocopy shop. But mostly you'll need *other people.* The more people you can get to try the experiments with you, the truer your results will be. (Don't forget to try them on yourself!) And the more experiments you do, the more people will start talking and listening and looking at different points of view. So you won't be the only person who learns from them.

Are You a Diver or a Wader?

Since the experimenter is part of every experiment, you need to check out some of your own attitudes and beliefs before you begin. They will shape the way you experiment as well as how you look at your results.

Check your "PSY-Q" by answering the following questions. For each question, choose the answer that is most like what you would do.

1. You have a new computer program. Do you figure it out by:
   A. sitting down and reading the instruction book, or
   B. popping the program into the computer and using what you already know, referring to the book only as a last resort?
2. Would you prefer to learn to swim by:
   A. taking formal lessons, or
   B. playing around in the water to get a feel for it?

3. Which do you think you would *never* forget:
   A. a poem you memorized, or
   B. how to ride a bicycle?
4. Are you more likely to keep working at a project where:
   A. you are supposed to find information and make a formal presentation, or
   B. you are working to satisfy your own curiosity because you truly want to learn something?
5. If you are crossing a street where there is no traffic, will you:
   A. walk the half-block to use the crosswalk because it's the law, or
   B. look both ways and cross in the middle?
6. When you learn to play a game that has long, complicated directions, do you:
   A. read through all the directions before beginning, or
   B. play with someone and learn the rules as you play?

What do your answers mean?

- If you chose more B answers than A answers, you are a *diver*. You are a trial-and-error sort of investigator who likes to learn by jumping right in and getting actively involved with your subject.
- If you chose more A answers than B answers, you are a *wader*. You would rather know exactly what you are going to do before you begin.

One way isn't necessarily better than the other, although it may work better at certain times and in certain circumstances. Both ways will give you information.

Whether you like to dive in or wade in, you'll find that *Psychology for Kids II* fits your style of investigation. How do you think a diver's experiments would differ from a wader's? What should each type of investigator be careful about? Might a diver miss an important detail? Might a wader waste valuable time? (For more on this subject, see "Do You Have a 'Spock' View or a 'Yoda' View?" on page 16.)

Your Obligations as an Experimenter

Before you start having fun with the experiments, please read and sign the Research Certificate on page 6. The certificate states your obligations as an experimenter. An obligation is a duty you have to behave in a responsible way. When you do experiments with other people or with animals—the subjects of your experiments—you agree to accept these obligations.

As a careful experimenter, you also need to keep track of your thoughts, expectations, experiences, results, and conclusions. You can do this with pencil and paper, or you can copy and use the Experiment Data Sheet on page 7. You will want to keep careful records for *every* experiment you do.

It's Official...

When you imagine an experimenter, what do you see? Someone hard at work in a laboratory, wearing a white coat and goggles? Someone surrounded by a lot of special equipment? Someone with a fancy degree? If so, you might be thinking, "I can't be an experimenter." Wrong!

Don't worry if your experiments aren't set up like "official" ones. If you are a less than perfect experimenter, you are in good company.

- Physicist Neils Bohr received the Nobel Prize for his description of the atom in the 1920s. Physicists have since decided that Bohr's description was wrong. Still, his model was accepted for over 50 years and was the basis for many important discoveries and inventions, including plastic. *(Tip:* The value of an experiment doesn't only depend on whether it's right or wrong, but also on the meaning we take from it.)
- Arthur Fleming returned from a vacation to find that he had forgotten to throw away some contaminated laboratory slides before leaving on his trip. He was getting rid of the mess when he noticed that the mold growing on the

slides was killing the bacteria. He had discovered penicillin, which has since saved many lives. (Fleming called it "mould juice.")

Happy accidents like Fleming's are called "serendipity." The word serendipity comes from a Persian tale about two princes from the land of Serendip around the year 420. The King of Serendip decided that his sons needed more education and that they had already learned all they could from books. So he sent them to explore the rest of the world in a hands-on sort of way...much like you will be doing when you try these experiments. The two princes had many adventures and made many discoveries by accident. They were always finding what they *weren't* looking for.

Going Beyond the Book

As you work your way through the experiments in this book, you may think of something else you'd like to investigate or try. Make a copy of the chart on page 8 and write your ideas there. That way you won't forget them. Eventually you'll have a list of potential new experiments.

As you gather information from the experiments, you may think of ways to use it in your daily life. Make a copy of the chart on page 9 and write your ideas there. Share them with your friends.

Whenever you add an idea to one of the charts, be sure to write the date when you had the idea and the number of the experiment you were doing at the time. Review your charts every once in awhile and choose an idea to follow up on. Be sure to note when and if you follow up on an idea.

Psychology for Kids

1. How can this information help me in a practical way?
2. How does it change my thinking?
3. How does it shape my actions?
4. What else do these results suggest?
5. What else does this make me want to explore?
6. What else might have caused these results?
7. What is the simplest explanation of these results?

Make Your Own Experimenter's Bookmark

1. Photocopy this page.
2. On your photocopy, cut out the strip at the left.
3. Laminate the strip at a copy shop, or glue it onto heavier paper (such as a file folder or posterboard).
4. Trim the edges.

You now have an Experimenter's Bookmark. Use it to mark your place in *Psychology for Kids II*. When you are finished doing the experiments, you might want to use your bookmark in your science book.

Tip: If you photocopy your bookmark on card stock, you won't have to laminate or glue it.

Make Your Own Experiments

- Do a lot of observing. Keep your eyes and ears open when you're waiting in lines, shopping, or eating in the school cafeteria. You'll probably get good ideas for things you want to explore.
- Ideas for experiments often begin with the thought, "Why do people...?" Do a lot of wondering and "what-if" thinking. Soon you will come up with ways to find answers to your questions.
- Once you have your basic idea, expand it by thinking about which groups you might compare: adults to children, right-handers to left-handers, males to females, city dwellers to rural residents, teachers to students, mail carriers to bank tellers (or any two occupations), publicly educated students to privately educated ones....the list is endless.
- If you have a copy of the original *Psychology for Kids,* you may want to turn some of the self-tests in that book into experiments to try on other people. Amy Geyer, a high school student in Little Falls, Minnesota, took Personal Style Inventory #34, "What's Your Learning Style?," from *Psychology for Kids* and turned it into an experiment called "Learning Styles of Children: Which Group Dominates Little Falls Community Schools?" As you sharpen your experimenter's skills, you'll find that you can turn almost any question into an experiment that gives interesting results.

RESEARCH CERTIFICATE

1. I will not do anything to other people that I wouldn't let them do to me.

2. I will make sure that everyone who takes part in my experiments knows what I am doing, why I am doing it, and what their role is. They will be fully informed, and I will obtain their oral or written agreement to be part of the experiment.

Exception: In some cases, explaining everything at the beginning can affect your results and wreck the experiment. In these cases, you will have to tell your subjects that you can't let them know everything at the start of the experiment, but you will when the experiment is over.

3. I will explain that everyone who agrees to take part in an experiment can stop it or drop out any time they want to.

4. I will never do anything to make anyone look stupid or foolish.

5. I will never do anything that will harm people or animals. I will take good care of animals during the experiments and return them to their natural environments when the experiments are over.

6. I will protect the privacy of my subjects.

7. At the end of an experiment, I will thank my subjects for their time and tell them everything they don't already know about the experiment. I will report to my subjects the actual methods and results of the experiment, and I will offer to answer any questions they might have about the experiment.

SIGNED ______________________________ DATE ________________________

EXPERIMENT DATA SHEET

TITLE OF EXPERIMENT: ______________________________

DATE BEGUN: ____________________ DATE ENDED: ____________________

WHAT I AM TRYING TO FIND OUT: ______________________________

WHAT I *EXPECTED* TO HAPPEN: ______________________________

WHAT *REALLY* HAPPENED: ______________________________

STATISTICAL RESULTS (HOW MANY? HOW FAR? HOW LONG? ETC.): ______________________________

COMMENTS/FEEDBACK FROM EXPERIMENT SUBJECTS: ______________________________

ANY SPECIAL CONDITIONS THAT MAY HAVE INFLUENCED THE RESULTS OF MY EXPERIMENT: ______________________________

CONCLUSIONS: WHAT DO MY RESULTS SUGGEST? ______________________________

HOW WOULD I DO THE EXPERIMENT DIFFERENTLY NEXT TIME? ______________________________

WHAT SPECIAL/UNEXPECTED PROBLEMS CAME UP THIS TIME? HOW CAN I AVOID THEM NEXT TIME? ______________________________

HAVE I MET MY OBLIGATIONS AS AN EXPERIMENTER, AS STATED ON MY RESEARCH CERTIFICATE? ______________________________

IDEAS FOR MORE EXPERIMENTS

DATE	IDEA	EXPERIMENT #	FOLLOW UP?

POSSIBLE USES IN MY DAILY LIFE

DATE	IDEA	EXPERIMENT #	FOLLOW UP?

A Special Note to Parents and Teachers

The experiments in *Psychology for Kids II* are all based on psychological theories and research. But this is not a book about the scientific method. These experiments are not meant to "prove" something, nor do they meet the rigorous standards of official experiments.

A "real" experiment requires resources and skills beyond the level of most readers of this book. A few of the things a scientifically planned experiment would require are:

- large numbers of subjects for each experiment,
- subjects selected at random from the population,
- a good working knowledge of statistics, and
- highly sophisticated timing and measuring devices and other equipment.

Students would need to become familiar with terms such as:

- control group,
- variable (and intervening variable), and
- standard deviation.

Even "real" scientific experiments often fail because of the many things that can go wrong.

In other words, the goal of this book is not a scientific one, although some important concepts of experimenting will be introduced. Rather, the goal of this book is to encourage students to interact in new ways with the people around them. Through the experiments in *Psychology for Kids II*, young people will:

- listen to their parents in new ways,
- learn how students are responsible for teachers making extra rules,
- look at the world from the point of view of a little kid,
- talk with adults in ways they normally wouldn't have the opportunity to do, because they will be discussing opinions, beliefs, and ideas, and
- become more aware of their surroundings and their own role as they participate in and observe what is going on around them.

Finally, *Psychology for Kids II* is meant to stir an interest in the subject of academic psychology at the elementary and middle school level and to encourage more students to pursue psychology at the high school level. Human behavior is at the core of virtually all problems and solutions. Bright, curious, committed young people are needed to propel the field forward. Self-esteem courses and programs—considered by some to be "psychology"—are sometimes seen at the elementary school level, but real academic experimental psychology is rare at this level. This is an omission I have tried to address with *Psychology for Kids II.*

I want to emphasize that this is not a "touchy-feely" book. It deals with attitudes, opinions, behaviors, and feelings, but on a different level than is usually found. Math, science, language, and the study of other cultures can easily be taught with and through these experiments. Results can be tabulated and graphed to teach math in a more meaningful way. The importance and impact of language is made clear through many of the experiments. And because these are experiments, they can be used to teach scientific methods and procedures of meticulous data gathering and measurement. The uses are limited only by your own imagination. Here are a few suggestions for working *Psychology for Kids II* into a curriculum:

- Start the New Year with **Experiment #9: Are Opinions Influenced by First Impressions?** and talk about how good it is to have a "clean slate."
- Dr. Martin Luther King believed in the power of cooperation to accomplish great things. To celebrate his spirit, try **Experiment #24: Are Some People More Cooperative than Others?**
- For Presidents' Day, you might want to explore **Experiment #7: What Are People's Attitudes about Money?**
- For April Fool's Day, look at **Experiment #4: How Easily Are People Fooled?**
- A discussion of self-fulfilling prophecies might be appropriate for a Friday the 13th. Start it off with **Experiment #1: Do People Get What They Expect?**
- The spring holidays are about hope and renewal. Plants come back to life, and we feel renewed, too. This might be a good time to get next to nature by doing **Experiment #33: What Can We Learn from Mealworms?**
- Are you looking for a Halloween activity that is different and more educational than most? Try **Experiment #29: Are We More Alike or More Different?** This special guest experiment is a search for the "perfect" apple...what better place to look than in the bobbing barrel? Or gather those Halloween pumpkins (before they are carved) and look for the perfect one.
- For Thanksgiving, try **Experiment #26: How Do Individuals Come Together as a Group?**
- A good experiment for the December holidays is **Experiment #5: Do People of Different Ages Have Different Views of Life?** Students may explore how they used to experience the holidays compared to how they experience them as they get older. They can also compare how they experience them to how their parents or busy shopkeepers might experience them.

There are more ways to use the experiments, but the most important thing *Psychology for Kids II* has to offer is the opportunity for children and adults to connect in a meaningful way. Young experimenters learn more about other people as they express their own opinions and listen to others' points of view. This is not only the key to self-understanding, but it is the one sure path to a more promising future for the human race.

A Resource for Those Interested in Teaching Psychology

The Psychology Special Interest Group (Psychology S.I.G.) is an official organization within the National Council for the Social Studies. The purpose of the Psychology S.I.G. is to encourage awareness of the field of psychology at the pre-college level. Membership dues at this writing are $15 for three years. Members receive newsletters during the year which contain teaching techniques, teaching strategies, and resources, all relating to the teaching of psychology. The newsletter also keeps members informed of state, regional, and national conventions related to the teaching of psychology—great places to meet and communicate with others who are teaching psychology. To find out more about the Psychology S.I.G. and the newsletter, contact one of the following individuals:

Jim Matiya
Carl Sandburg High School
131st and La Grange Road
Orland Park, IL 60462

Dale Kinney
Ralston High School
90th and Park Drive
Omaha, NE 68127

WHAT DO EXPERIMENTS DO?

Do People Get What They Expect?

What kinds of results do experimenters get from their experiments? You might think that this always depends on the experiment, or the people or materials involved, or some combination of those factors. In fact, experimenters often get the results they expect! This phenomenon is usually called a "self-fulfilling prophecy" or "the Rosenthal Effect." This experiment explores how attitudes can determine results.

SUBJECTS

- 5 kids in first or second grade
- 10 kids in fifth or sixth grade, divided into 2 groups of 5 (Group A and Group B)

WHAT YOU NEED

- 4 assistants
- 5 balls
- Paper and pencil for recording observations and results, or a copy of the Experiment Data Sheet on page 7

WHAT TO DO

Do this experiment first with Group A, then with Group B. Each group will play catch with the same group of younger kids for 5 minutes. Groups A and B should not be able to see or hear each other while the experiment is going on.

1. Tell Group A that you want them to play catch for a few minutes with some younger kids who have good athletic abilities. Have your assistants observe each pair playing catch. Have them count the number of times the younger kids miss the ball.
2. Tell Group B that you want them to play catch for a few minutes with some younger kids who may be rather clumsy. Again, have your assistants observe and count the misses.
3. Ask both groups of older kids what they thought of the ability of the younger kids they played catch with.
4. Ask the younger kids which group of older kids was the most fun to play catch with.

CONCLUSIONS

- Did the younger kids perform any differently when the older kids believed they were clumsy?
- Did expectations ("these kids are athletic" vs. "these kids are clumsy") influence the way people felt about each other?

EXPLORE MORE

- Choose any experiment in this book and have two different people try it. Tell one of them to expect a certain kind of result. Tell the other person to expect the opposite result.

WHY IT MATTERS TO YOU

- When you expect people to like you, they often do. Your expectation makes you act in more likable ways.
- When someone expects you to be kind, you are more likely to respond with kindness than when someone is worried that you will be mean or rude.
- Remind yourself to look at expectations. Ask yourself, "What did I expect to get on this test?" "What did I expect my brother to say or do?" "What did the other person expect me to think or do?" These types of questions will clue you in to the attitudes that were present at the beginning of a situation and likely played a part in what actually happened.
- Pay attention to this experimental effect when you are trying to succeed at something. Imagine that two people are starting out to do something difficult. One expects to fail; the other expects to succeed. Both experience little failures along the way. But the one who expects to fail eventually gives up, thinking, "I *knew* I would fail!" The one who expects to succeed learns from the little failures and keeps moving toward the goal.

DID YOU KNOW?

- In one experiment, students took an intelligence test. Afterward, some teachers were told that certain students had scored high on the test and would make remarkable gains in their intellectual development during the next 8 months. In fact, the students had not scored especially high on the test—no higher than many other students. The only real difference between them and the other students was *in the minds of the teachers*

  At the end of the school year, the students were given the same intelligence test they had taken at the beginning of the school year. The "bright" students had gained 4 points more, on average, than the other students.

  When teachers were asked to describe the "bright" students, they used words like "happier," "more curious," and "more interesting." Other students who also gained points but who weren't "supposed to" (because they hadn't been in the "bright" group) were described by the teachers as "less affectionate," "less well-adjusted," and "less interesting."
- The Rosenthal Effect works on animals as well as people. Two groups of experimenters were working with rats. One group was told that their rats were "bright." The other group was told that their rats were "dull." The "bright" rats actually performed better in experiments than the "dull" rats.

Do You Have a "Spock" View or a "Yoda" View?

Do you believe that human behavior is—or should be—logical and controllable? Or do you believe that humans are mysterious creatures who reach out into the universe and use "the Force"? These are two basic views of human behavior and human nature.

What you believe about humans will influence your experiments. Take some time to think about your attitudes before doing any more experiments. Answer A or B depending on which statement you agree with more.

1. A. Humans are controlled by forces outside of their control.
B. Humans are responsible for their own actions.

2. A. Humans can be studied only by observing what they do.
B. Humans can be studied by asking them what they think and/or feel.

3. A. Humans are predictable.
B. Humans are not predictable.

4. A. Humans have no free will.
B. Humans have free will.

5. A. Humans mostly communicate existing information from one to another.
B. Humans mostly create new information.

6. A. It is most important to know about things.
B. It is most important to experience things.

7. A. Humans are not uniquc in the animal kingdom.
B. Humans are unique in the animal kingdom.

8. A. Truth is absolute (in other words, good is good and evil is evil).
B. Truth is relative (in other words, good and evil depend on the situation).

9. A. Life can best be understood by looking at its individual parts.
B. Life can best be understood by looking for patterns in the whole.

10. A. What is important is what exists.
B. What is important is what could be.

11. A. Scientific certainty is possible.
B. Scientific certainty is not possible.

12. A. The world is the same to everyone.
B. The world is experienced differently by each individual.

What do your answers mean?

- 10–12 A's or B's mean that you have a strong attitude one way or the other about human nature. The stronger your belief, the more likely it will influence your experiments
- A lot more A's than B's mean that you have a *Spock* view of human nature. You perceive humans more as machines which can be completely understood. You tend to think that human behavior can, at least in theory, be totally predicted and programmed.
- A lot more B's than A's mean that you have a *Yoda* view of human nature. You perceive humans as free spirits who can't quite be defined or completely understood by science.

How might each attitude influence experimentation? Might a Spock be more interested in experiments testing reactions that can be measured physically? Might a Yoda be more excited about experiments that explore people's attitudes and relationships?

Do People Change When They Are Part of an Experiment?

When people are aware that they are part of an experiment, they may not act as they would in a real-life situation. This experiment suggests that people may try to make things seem as "normal" as possible, even without being aware of what they are doing.

SUBJECTS

- 6 people

WHAT YOU NEED

- A copy of Picture of a Man from page 19 (mask the Picture of a Spaceship so only Picture of a Man shows on your copy)
- Paper and pencils for your subjects
- Paper and pencil for recording observations and results, or a copy of the Experiment Data Sheet on page 7

WHAT TO DO

1. Show your first subject the Picture of a Man. Let your subject look at the picture for about 10 seconds before you take it away. Then have the person draw the picture from memory and write the title "Picture of a Man" at the bottom.
2. Show your second subject the picture your *first* subject drew. Don't let your second subject see the original picture from this book. Again, have the person draw the picture from memory and write the title at the bottom.
3. Show your third subject the picture your *second* subject drew. Have the person draw the picture from memory.
4. Continue in this way with your fourth, fifth, and sixth subjects, showing each person only the drawing made by the subject right before him or her.

CONCLUSIONS

- Did the drawings get more and more "normal" looking?
- How might the desire to make things seem "normal" change an experiment as subjects try to guess what the experiment is about?

EXPLORE MORE

- Try this experiment with more than 6 people. Do you find a point at which the drawings stop changing as much? In other words, after the picture gets "normal enough," does it show less change?
- Try a similar experiment using a nonsense sentence, whispered from one person to the next (as in the game of "Telephone" or "Gossip"). Does a nonsense sentence eventually make sense? *Example:* "Gurgles are dutiful" might become "Girls are beautiful."
- Repeat the experiment with the Picture of a Spaceship on page 19. (It's the same illustration as before, turned upside-down and given a new title.) Do your subjects draw it more and more

to look like a spaceship? Compare their drawings to the ones from the Picture of a Man experiment. Do you think the titles influenced how your subjects recalled each picture? If so, how?

- Repeat the Picture of a Man experiment, only this time tell some of your subjects the purpose of the experiment ahead of time. Are the results different?
- Repeat the Picture of a Man experiment with several groups. Tell each group the purpose of the experiment ahead of time—only give each group a *different* purpose. *Examples:* "This experiment tests your memory." "This experiment tests your artistic ability." "This experiment tests your creative ability." Are the results different from one group to another? If so, how are they different?

WHY IT MATTERS TO YOU

- People often fail to remember something because they didn't really observe it in the first place. If you pay close attention in class, you probably won't need to spend so much time studying. Paying attention improves your memory.
- When you do experiments, you learn to be a very good observer.

DID YOU KNOW?

- You don't necessarily remember something the way it really happened. The words used to describe an event will influence the way you remember it later on. *Examples:* "That was a horrible scary movie." "That was a really fun scary movie."
- How an experiment is explained or presented to subjects can influence and even change the results.

The Powers of Observation

People see the same things at the same time...but differently.

An experiment is a carefully controlled observation. You can see for yourself how two people perceive external reality in different ways by doing a careful, but uncontrolled, observation.

Observe something for a few minutes—an anthill, ducks in a pond, kittens playing, kids shooting baskets. Write down everything your senses perceive. If there is a breeze blowing a few grains of sand, write it down. If a truck goes by with a loud rumble and squeaky brakes, make a note.

Meanwhile, have a friend observe the same thing you are observing. Then, after a few minutes, compare your notes. Chances are they will not be exactly alike. What is one possible explanation you can think of for this?

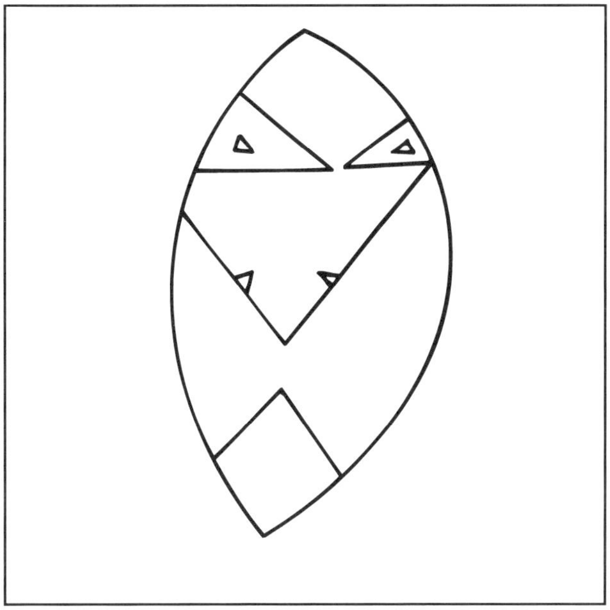

PICTURE OF A MAN

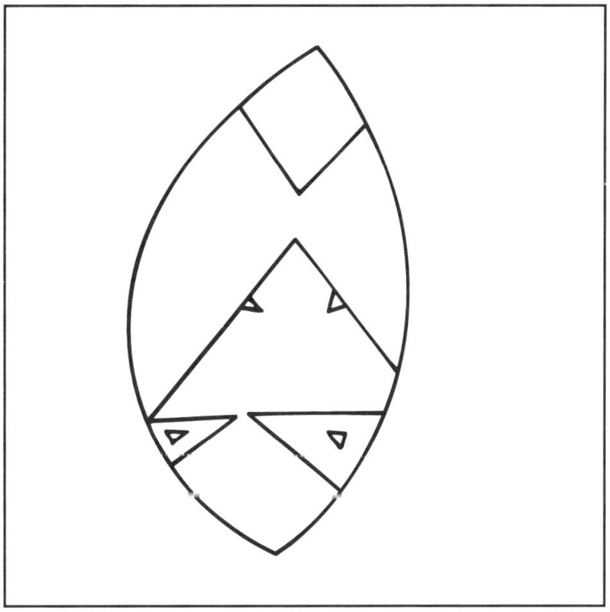

PICTURE OF A SPACESHIP

Are People More Logical or More Emotional?

Every experiment is affected by the beliefs and attitudes of the subjects. That is why it helps to learn more about the basic beliefs of the average person. For example, are people more logical or more emotional? If they are more logical, you should be able to predict their choices in this experiment—and maybe in other experiments, too.

SUBJECTS

- 3 or more people

WHAT YOU NEED

- An assistant
- A deck of playing cards
- 52 tokens, such as pennies or buttons
- Paper and pencil for tallying responses; divide the paper into 4 columns labeled "Hearts," "Spades," "Clubs," and "Diamonds" (you will need one tally page for each subject)
- Paper and pencil for recording observations and results, or a copy of the Experiment Data Sheet on page 7

WHAT TO DO

Do this experiment with one subject at a time.

1. Put the tokens in a pile in the middle of the table.
2. Explain that you will be turning over the cards in a deck, one at a time. Say, "Before I turn over each card, tell me if it will be a heart or not a heart. Each time you are right, you will take a token. Each time you are wrong, you will give me a token."
3. Go through the whole deck. Have your assistant tally the responses as they are given by checking the columns on the tally sheet.

Repeat steps 1–3 for each of your other subjects.

CONCLUSIONS

- What proportion of the time did your subjects choose hearts?
- How do you explain this behavior?
- How do your subjects explain it? Ask them. How many tried to figure out mathematically how often hearts would come up? How many chose hearts because it "felt" right?
- Do you find that people use their logic more or their feelings more? *Hint:* If your subjects use logic, they may choose hearts 1/4 of the time because 1/4 of the deck is hearts.

EXPLORE MORE

- Try the same experiment with subjects of different ages, genders, and occupations.
- Would you expect an engineer to perform any differently than an artist? Why or why not?

WHY IT MATTERS TO YOU

- Because people are generally not totally logical in their fears, hopes, and dreams, they may not always act the way you think they will.
- Make your own "logic checks" from time to time to keep track of your fears, hopes, and dreams. This will help you to be realistic...a good way to avoid feeling disappointed! *Examples*: Should you be disappointed if you don't get 20 home runs in a row? Check out how many professionals do that well. Should you worry about getting a terrible disease? Look up the real statistics. Most often, you will find this information comforting.

DID YOU KNOW?

- Your chances of winning a lottery are about 1 in 4 million.
- Your chances of being killed in an airplane crash are 1 in 4,600,000.
- Your chances of being killed in a car crash are 1 in 125.

Yet people continue to play the lottery, and most believe that airplane trips are more risky than car trips.

What about you?

ATTITUDES AND BELIEFS

How Easily Are People Fooled?

People often believe what they want to believe. They believe what makes them feel good, or what fits best with what they already believe. This experiment explores what sometimes happens because of this.

SUBJECTS

- 3 or more people

WHAT YOU NEED

- Copies of the Personality Test on page 27, one for each subject
- Pencils for your subjects
- Paper and pencil for recording observations and results, or a copy of the Experiment Data Sheet on page 7

WHAT TO DO

1. Ask each subject to take the Personality Test. Have them tell you what they see in each of the three inkblots.
2. Afterward, pretend to look up the meaning of their answers in this book. Read the Fake Personality Profile to each person separately (without the real title, of course). Afterward, ask, "How well does this description seem to fit you?"

Fake Personality Profile

You have a strong need to be admired and liked. You tend to be critical of yourself when you don't need to be. You have a lot of potential that you could use to your advantage, but you are currently wasting it on idle fun.

You have some personality weaknesses, but you are able to hide them quite well. You usually appear calm and in control on the outside, even when you are feeling worried and insecure. At times, you worry that you have made wrong decisions or you have not done the "right" thing.

You don't like to have your freedom tied up with all sorts of silly rules. If someone wants to change your mind, they'd better have proof that they're right, because you're a person who likes to think for yourself.

You like a certain amount of change and variety in your life. Though you are sociable at times, you also have a need for privacy and quiet.

Sometimes you feel that everyone else just doesn't "get it." At other times you feel like you're the only one who doesn't fit in and everyone else "gets it."

Some of your hopes for your future success might seem self-centered and unrealistic.

CONCLUSIONS

- What's wrong with the Fake Personality Profile?
- Why are people fooled by descriptions like this one? (The descriptions are very general. Most of us fill in any missing information with our own ideas about ourselves.)

If your subjects agreed with this "one-size-fits all" description, it's because it's very general and describes feelings that most people have about themselves at one time or another. *Examples:*

1. "You have a strong need to be admired and liked." (Nearly everyone has this need.)
2. "You tend to be critical of yourself when you don't need to be." (Nearly everyone does this.)
3. "You have a lot of potential that you could use to your advantage, but you are currently wasting it on idle fun." (Who doesn't do this at least some of the time?)
4. "You have some personality weaknesses, but you are able to hide them quite well." (Key word: SOME. We like to at least *think* that we can hide our weaknesses.)
5. "You usually appear calm and in control on the outside, even when you are feeling worried and insecure." (Key word: USUALLY.)
6. "At times, you worry that you have made wrong decisions or you have not done the 'right' thing." (Key words: AT TIMES. Nearly everybody worries about this at times.)
7. "You don't like to have your freedom tied up with all sorts of silly rules." (Imagine someone saying, "You know, what I *really* enjoy about life is having my freedom tied up with all sorts of silly rules." Not very likely.)
8. "You're a person who likes to think for yourself." (Even those of us who don't really think for ourselves like to *think* that we think for ourselves.)
9. "You like a certain amount of change and variety in your life." (Key words: CERTAIN AMOUNT. It would be rare for someone to want *no* change and *no* variety in life.)
10. "Though you are sociable at times, you also have a need for privacy and quiet." (Key words: AT TIMES. Few people would never/always want to be sociable or never/always want privacy.)
11. "Sometimes you feel that everyone else just doesn't 'get it.' At other times you feel like you're the only one who doesn't fit in and everyone else 'gets it.'" (If you can't identify the key words by now, you're not paying attention!)
12. "Some of your hopes for your future success might seem self-centered and unrealistic." (Is there anyone who has *never* been self-centered? Who has *never* had unrealistic hopes? I hope not!)

- What makes people want to believe that someone else can tell them about themselves or their future? Why don't they believe their own evaluation of themselves as much—or more?

EXPLORE MORE

- Make up your own meaningless Personality Test with shapes or pictures. Then make up your own Fake Personality Profile. See if you can write it in such a way that *anybody* would believe that it describes him or her.

WHY IT MATTERS TO YOU

People easily believe nonsense they are told about themselves. Knowing this should remind you to be cautious about:

- believing any sort of gossip or rumors about other people
- believing something bad about yourself
- believing in nonscientific things that supposedly tell you about yourself, such as horoscopes or fortune tellers.

DID YOU KNOW?

Fortune tellers use psychological tricks to fool people into thinking they know the future. But what they *really* know is how to speak very generally and how to get information about people without the people knowing it. Here are some of their tricks:

- They tell all young men that they are attractive to young women.
- They tell unhappy-looking women that soon they will have fights with their husbands.
- If the person looks puzzled by what the fortune teller is saying, the fortune teller changes directions. *Example:* A fortune teller says to you, "I see your brother...." You look puzzled; you don't have a brother. Meanwhile, the fortune teller says, "No, wait, I mean your sister, or maybe just a girl you know...." If you don't look puzzled, the fortune teller continues along the same line.

PERSONALITY TEST

Look at each inkblot. What do you see?

1.

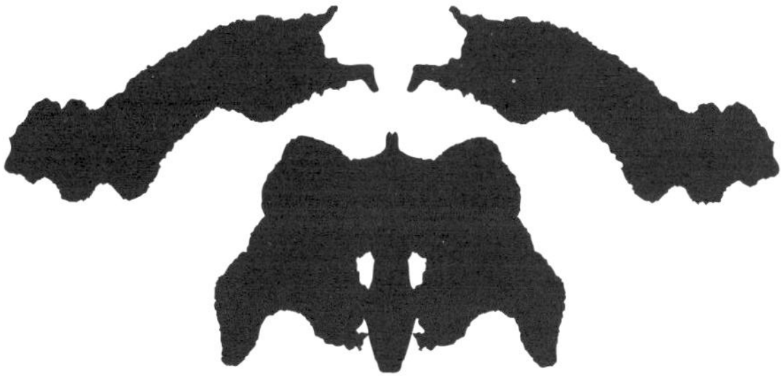

2.

3.

Do People of Different Ages Have Different Views of Life?

Life is one giant experiment. You learn as you live. Different "lessons" or discoveries may seem more important at different ages and stages of life. This experiment helps you to see how the things that matter change as we live and learn from the big experiment we call "life."

SUBJECTS

- Any number of people of different ages (the bigger the gap between youngest and oldest, the better)

WHAT YOU NEED

- Copies of the How Old? test on page 30, one for each subject
- Pencils for your subjects
- Paper and pencil for recording observations and results, or a copy of the Experiment Data Sheet on page 7

WHAT TO DO

1. Introduce the How Old? test by saying, "The quotations on this test are from people of different ages, from 6 to 81."
2. Have your subjects complete the test.
3. Check their answers. Correct any wrong answers. Give them the right answers.

Answers

1. 19
2. 7
3. 51
4. 81
5. 7
6. 66
7. 6

CONCLUSIONS

Your subjects probably were able to guess which quotations were said by 6- and 7-year-olds.

- How do views of younger people differ from views of older people?
- Is a younger person always easier to spot than an older person?
- What do the responses of older people have in common?

EXPLORE MORE

- Create your own survey to find out what people of different ages have learned from life. Or make up one question to ask people of different age groups, genders, occupations, etc., then compare their perceptions. *Example:* "How do you perceive birthdays?"
- Children often pretend to do grown-up things. See if you can talk some grown-ups into doing some things they have not done since they were children, such as swinging on a swing, playing hopscotch, or skipping. Afterward, ask, "How did you feel about (swinging, playing hopscotch, skipping)? Did you feel differently about it when you were a child?"

WHY IT MATTERS TO YOU

- Think about the life lessons you have learned so far. Which one is the most important?
- As different situations (good and bad) occur in your life, it helps to see them as lessons. You are less likely to repeat mistakes and more likely to repeat successes. Bad or unpleasant situations are easier to get through when your suffering seems purposeful rather than pointless.

DID YOU KNOW?

- Feelings play a big role in how you see what you see. Strangers look alike, but friends look unique. Middle school looks big when you are in third grade, but smaller when you return as a high school senior to visit your former teacher. An egg for breakfast may sound good until your little brother starts talking about where eggs come from.

HOW OLD?

The 7 quotations on this page are from 7 different people. Their ages are:

6 7 7 19 51 66 81

As you read the quotations, match each one with an age.

_____ **1.** "I've learned that if there were no problems there would be no opportunities."

_____ **2.** "I've learned that you can't hide a piece of broccoli in a glass of milk."

_____ **3.** "I've learned that everyone has something to teach."

_____ **4.** "I've learned that if you smile at people they will almost always smile back."

_____ **5.** "I've learned that if you laugh and drink soda pop at the same time, it will come out of your nose."

_____ **6.** "I've learned that whenever I decide something with kindness, I usually make the right decision."

_____ **7.** "I've learned that if you spread the peas out on your plate, it looks like you ate more."

The quotations are from *Live and Learn and Pass It On* by H. Jackson Brown, Jr. (Nashville, TN: Rutledge Hill Press, 1992). If you want to read more, visit your library or bookstore.

How Do Young Children View the Physical World?

Do you ever think back to when you were younger and wonder, "How could I ever have done or believed *that?*" This experiment helps you to find out why things seem so different to you now than they did back then. Young children actually think differently and have their own special logic. One day in the future, you may even look back to today and wonder, "How could I ever have done or believed *that?*"

SUBJECTS

- A 3-year-old
- A 5-year-old

WHAT YOU NEED

- Copies of the Faces, Stars, and Rain pictures on page 33
- 2 clear drinking glasses—1 short and fat, 1 tall and thin
- A bowl of water and a dipper
- Paper and pencil for recording observations and results, or a copy of the Experiment Data Sheet on page 7

WHAT TO DO

Do this experiment with one subject at a time.

1. Start by finding out if the child knows the difference between MORE and LESS by asking these questions:
   - "Would you rather have MORE fun or LESS fun?"
   - "Would you rather have MORE yummy food or LESS yummy food?"

   Show the Faces picture and ask:
   - "Which person is LESS happy?"

   Show the Stars picture and ask:
   - "Which box has MORE stars?"

   Show the Rain picture and ask:
   - "Which picture has LESS rain?"

   The child who can answer these questions correctly probably knows the difference between MORE and LESS.
2. Use the dipper to fill the short glass half full. Then have the child watch closely as you pour the water from the short glass into the tall glass. Ask:
   - "Is there MORE water now, LESS water, or the SAME AMOUNT of water?"
3. Empty the glasses. Then have the child put one dipper full of water into each glass. Ask:
   - "Into which glass did you put MORE water?"

CONCLUSIONS

- When the child dips water into both glasses, he or she should realize that both glasses contain the same amount...right? That seems reasonable to expect. But does it really happen?

EXPLORE MORE

- Repeat steps 2 and 3 of the experiment with another 5-year-old—one who didn't see you do the experiment with the first 5-year-old. If the child correctly tells you that each glass has the same amount of water, ask, "How do you know?"
- Experiment with more children of different ages. For best results, try to find several 3-year-olds and several 5-year-olds. Tally and compare your results.

WHY IT MATTERS TO YOU

- How might you behave differently if you didn't know what you know about the physical world? *Example:* Do you think you might be more likely to jump from a rooftop?
- When you are around young children, try to remember that they aren't just smaller versions of you and your friends. They really do see the world in a very different way, and something that is pretend to you may seem real to them.

Children's Logic

Jean Piaget, a famous Swiss psychologist, found that 3-year-olds usually think there is more water in a tall, skinny glass than in a short, fat glass, even when they see that same water poured from a fat glass into a skinny glass. (Did you make the same discovery in your experiment?)

More recent studies of children's thinking find that children are more logical than Piaget's studies suggested. For instance, when a 4-year-old was asked, "Can a rock walk?," the child answered, "No." Why not? "Because the rock has no legs." When the child was asked, "Can a doll walk?," the child again answered, "No." Why not? "Because the doll's legs are pretend."

In one study, a child was told to call a dog by the word "cow." When the experimenter asked, "Does a cow have horns?," the child said, "Of course, if a dog is called a cow, then there must be horns. Such a dog, which is called cow, must have little horns."

Sometimes when adults ask children "dumb" questions in experiments, the children respond with equally nutty answers, purely in fun. They may think that the adult is just playing a game with them. How might this affect the results of an experiment?

What Are People's Attitudes about Money?

The attitudes people have about money can give you a clue to what they think is more important in life—to *do* or to *have.* This experiment explores some of the ways in which people view money and its uses.

SUBJECTS

- As many people as you want to test

WHAT YOU NEED

- Copies of the What Would You Do with $5,000? questionnaire on page 36, one for each subject
- Pencils for your subjects
- Paper and pencil for tallying responses; head one piece of paper "Male Subjects," the other "Female Subjects," and divide each paper into columns numbered 1–10 (for the questions on the questionnaire)
- Paper and pencil for recording observations and results, or a copy of the Experiment Data Sheet on page 7

WHAT TO DO

1. Give each subject a copy of the What Would You Do with $5,000? questionnaire.
2. Collect the completed questionnaires and tally the responses.

CONCLUSIONS

- Subjects who checked more of the ODD numbered items prefer to spend their money on experiences. Subjects who checked more of the EVEN numbered items prefer to have their money in a concrete form—they want actual objects or actual money.
- Do more of your subjects seem to want to spend their money on experiences or on objects?

EXPLORE MORE

- Compare the responses of your male subjects and your female subjects. Can you draw any conclusions?
- Change the first line on the questionnaire to read, "You have SAVED $5,000.00" (instead of "You have WON $5,000.00"). Then try it out on more subjects and tally responses. Are the responses different when the money is saved than when the money is won?
- Do a survey to find out what people dream of doing with money if they ever win a big amount. Ask questions like, "Would you quit your job?" "Would you move to another place?" "What would you buy first?" "Would you give some of your money away?"
- Consider your own attitudes about money. Where did you get those attitudes?

WHY IT MATTERS TO YOU

- Different people have very different "rules" about money—about borrowing it, saving it, spending it, lending it. The more you can find out about how the people in your life feel about money, and the more alike your "rules" are, the better you will get along.
- Most people don't think of their attitudes about money as "attitudes." They tend to think of them as "facts." Check this out with a simple survey. Ask several people (including family members), "What is money?" Their responses may be very different, and each person will firmly believe that his or her answer is the right one.

DID YOU KNOW?

- One major source of disagreement in many marriages and friendships is money—what to do with it, or even worse, what to do without it!
- Often, when countries go to war, it is over economic issues as much as (or more than) philosophical issues.

WHAT WOULD YOU DO WITH $5,000?

You have won $5,000.00.
You may spend it on anything listed here.
You must choose exactly *5 different items.*
Put a check mark beside each of your choices.

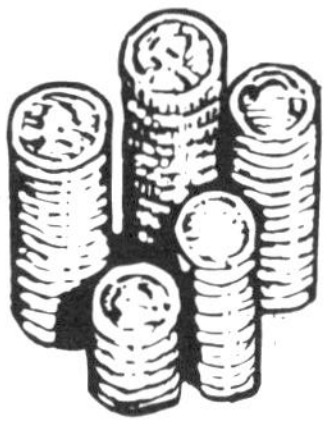

___ **1.** Dinners at fancy restaurants

___ **2.** Clothing

___ **3.** Travel/vacations

___ **4.** Your savings account

___ **5.** Music or sports events (concerts, baseball games, ballets, basketball games, etc.)

___ **6.** Works of art/posters

___ **7.** Games/athletic equipment (video games, computer games, bicycles, skis, skates, etc.)

___ **8.** Stereo equipment

___ **9.** Classes/training (exercise, recreational, or educational)

___ **10.** Jewelry

Check one:

I am ____ male ____ female

OPINIONS AND JUDGMENTS

Can One Negative Word Change an Opinion?

Imagine this: You get back a school paper you worked very hard on and find a big A at the top. In addition, your teacher has written comments throughout your paper. You find nine positive comments ("good idea," "great examples," etc.) But you also find one negative comment ("watch your spelling" or "a bit dull right here"). How much do you think the single negative comment will change how you feel about your A? This experiment explores how a single negative word can change an overall big picture that is otherwise positive.

SUBJECTS

- 2 groups of people (Group A and Group B), with the same number in each group (the more the better)

WHAT YOU NEED

- Copies of the pictures on pages 40–43—one set of A pictures for each person in Group A, and one set of B pictures for each person in Group B
- Paper and pencils for your subjects
- Paper and pencil for recording observations and results, or a copy of the Experiment Data Sheet on page 7

WHAT TO DO

There are 4 pictures, 2 each of 2 different people. Notice that one version of each picture includes a list of all *positive* words. The other version includes almost the same list, but with one *negative* word.

1. Give everyone in Group A copies of pictures A-1 and A-2. Give everyone in Group B copies of pictures B-1 and B-2.
2. Ask your subjects to write a short description of the life of each person shown in the pictures. They should include the person's occupation, type of neighborhood, hobbies and interests, type of car, etc.

CONCLUSIONS

- Compare Group A's responses with Group B's responses. Did *one* negative word make a difference in how subjects judged the people in the pictures?

EXPLORE MORE

- Repeat the experiment with different word lists. You might use a list of all negative words and a list with one positive word. Does one positive word create a more favorable impression?

WHY IT MATTERS TO YOU

- It's important to realize that if you say even one negative word about someone, you may change the way others see him or her.
- On the other hand, if you can say something positive about a person, you may do more good than you know.

DID YOU KNOW?

- People who are liked and respected for one trait will be rated higher on other traits that are not as remarkable. This is called "the Halo Effect."
- A quotation attributed to Einstein would be given more weight than the same quotation attributed to a game show host or cartoon character. (You can turn this into another experiment.)

A-1

Skjold Photographs

SOCIABLE

IMPORTANT

GENEROUS

DISHONEST

HUMOROUS

IMAGINATIVE

A-2

Skjold Photographs

SOCIABLE

IMPORTANT

GENEROUS

RELIABLE

HUMOROUS

IMAGINATIVE

B-1

Skjold Photographs

SOCIABLE

IMPORTANT

GENEROUS

RELIABLE

HUMOROUS

IMAGINATIVE

B-2

Skjold Photographs

SOCIABLE

IMPORTANT

GENEROUS

DISHONEST

HUMOROUS

IMAGINATIVE

Are Opinions Influenced by First Impressions?

You know that facts help to form opinions. So if two reasonable people have the same facts, shouldn't they come up with the same opinion? Of course, this doesn't always happen, and this experiment may help to explain why. It suggests that opinions are shaped by the order in which facts are learned. Each fact sets up an expectation and shapes the meaning of the fact that follows it.

SUBJECTS

- 2 groups of 3 or more people (Group A and Group B)

WHAT YOU NEED

- Paper and pencil for recording responses; divide the paper into 5 columns labeled "Yes," "No," "Would Hire," "Wouldn't Hire," and "Reasons for Hiring/Not Hiring"
- Paper and pencil for recording observations and results, or a copy of the Experiment Data Sheet on page 7

WHAT TO DO

Do this experiment with one group at a time.

1. Start with Group A. Say, "I will read a list of 6 words describing someone. Then I will ask 3 questions about the person." Read the word list aloud. Pause for 2 seconds between each word.
    - intelligent
    - hard-working
    - aggressive
    - critical
    - stubborn
    - jealous

2. Ask Group A the following 3 questions. Record responses.
   - "Would you like to know such a person?"
   - "Would you hire such a person to work for you?"
   - "Why or why not?"
3. Repeat steps 1–2 for Group B, but use this list of words instead:
   - jealous
   - stubborn
   - critical
   - aggressive
   - hard-working
   - intelligent

CONCLUSIONS

- If first impressions influence opinions, you should find that the people in Group A rated the individual higher than the people in Group B.
- Notice that the two lists are identical, except that the words are listed in reverse order. For Group A, the positive words are listed first. For Group B, the negative words are listed first. Your experiment subjects might make a judgment about the person being described after hearing only the first few words on the list. By the time they hear the last few words, they have already decided if the person is "good" or "bad."

EXPLORE MORE

- Check your attitudes from time to time. Maybe you met someone you didn't like at first because you saw only the "bad side" and formed your opinion based on that. Maybe the person deserves another chance. Or maybe you became friends with someone whose "good side" you saw first, but now it doesn't feel like a real friendship. Take another look here, too.
- Sometimes people who seem hard to get to know are the most worth knowing.

WHY IT MATTERS TO YOU

- If you earn high grades on the first few tests or papers you do for a particular teacher, your chances of getting high grades on future assignments are a little higher. If, on the other hand, you earn average or low grades on the first few tests or papers, it will be slightly more difficult to get higher grades because you will have to overcome the "bad" first impression you made. *Tip:* Do your best at the beginning!
- If you have a plan to present or news to share, start with the "good" parts and save the "bad" parts for the end.
- If someone ever says to you, "I have good news and bad news. Which do you want to hear first?," always ask for the good news first. You'll feel more prepared to handle the bad news.

DID YOU KNOW?

- A newly hatched duckling will follow the first thing it sees after it is born, as if that object (or person, or animal) is its mother. This very powerful first impression is called "imprinting." It was researched by Konrad Lorenz.

How Do People Make Judgments?

Do people wait until all the facts are in before they make up their mind? Or do they gather pieces of information as they go along, like a snowball rolling across the ground gathers more snow? This experiment gives you one way to find out.

SUBJECTS

- 2 groups of people (Group A and Group B), with an equal number in each group

WHAT YOU NEED

- 2 pieces of paper with words written on them; on the first piece of paper, write ANGLE/ RECTANGLE/SQUARE/CIRCLE, on the second piece of paper, write CIRCLE/ RECTANGLE/SQUARE/ANGLE
- Paper and pencil for recording observations and results, or a copy of the Experiment Data Sheet on page 7

WHAT TO DO

Do this experiment with one group at a time.

1. Show Group A the paper with the words ANGLE/RECTANGLE/SQUARE/CIRCLE. Ask, "Which one doesn't go with the other three?"
2. Show Group B the paper with the words CIRCLE/RECTANGLE/SQUARE/ANGLE. Ask, "Which one doesn't go with the other three?"

CONCLUSIONS

- The subjects in Group A will probably say that CIRCLE doesn't belong. The subjects in Group B will probably say that ANGLE doesn't belong.

If this is what actually happens, it means that the subjects in each group were deciding about the list as they went along. Can you figure out how they reached their decisions? (The first list describes 3 angular shapes and then a round one. Therefore, CIRCLE doesn't belong. The second list describes 3 enclosed shapes and then an open one. Therefore, ANGLE doesn't belong.)

EXPLORE MORE

Ask someone the following riddle: "The word FOLK is pronounced with a silent 'L'—FOKE. The name POLK is pronounced with the 'L,' just like it's spelled. How do you pronounce the word that means the white of an egg?" Most people will respond with YOKE, for YOLK. But the yolk is actually the *yellow* part of an egg. The white is the ALBUMEN. Why do most people get this riddle wrong? Because they think of the answer as being part of a set with FOLK and POLK.

See if you can make up similar riddles.

WHY IT MATTERS TO YOU

People who have known you for a long time have a good idea of what you're really like. But this isn't true for strangers or people who haven't known you for very long—a fact most people tend to forget. As this experiment shows, opinions are formed *as we go along*, not after all the facts are in. While this may not seem fair, it's still true. Therefore, it's probably a good idea to be on your best behavior as much as possible, especially when you're getting to know new people.

DID YOU KNOW?

Salespeople can get customers to buy their products by setting them up with a series of questions. They start by asking questions that are likely to get "yes" answers." *Examples:* "Nice weather we're having, isn't it?" "Is that your little girl?" "Isn't that a great refrigerator?" Once the customer is used to saying "yes," the salesperson slips in the real question: "Would you like to have this refrigerator in your home?"

PERCEPTIONS

How Does the Brain Organize What We See?

Perception influences attitudes. When you learn certain things about perception, you start to understand why most people perceive their own opinions as facts. Healthy, happy relationships are based on people understanding each other's points of view. This is true for groups, communities, even whole countries. Respecting other people's viewpoints, and expecting them to value yours, is a positive, powerful way to relate to the world.

Although we all see different things, and we all see things differently, there are many rules of perception which seem to be universal. These general laws were discovered by a group of psychologists who studied how the brain organizes what it sees. The psychologists discovered that we tend to complete images that are incomplete and to organize what we see into patterns and groups. This experiment gives you a chance to share in their discovery.

SUBJECTS

- As many people as you want to test

WHAT YOU NEED

- Copies of the Visual Perception Test on page 53, one for each subject
- Copies of How Do You Rate Yourself? on page 54, one for each subject
- Pencils for your subjects
- Paper and pencil for recording observations and results, or a copy of the Experiment Data Sheet on page 7
- A timer (optional; for Explore More)
- Copies of the illusions on page 55 (optional; for Explore More)

WHAT TO DO

1. Have your subjects take the Visual Perception Test. Ask them to sign their tests. Collect the tests.
2. Next, have your subjects complete a How Do You Rate Yourself? form. Ask them to sign their forms. Collect the forms.

Typical Responses to Visual Perception Test

Section A:

1. Circle

2. Square

3. Arc with line through it

4. Two triangles

We have a natural tendency to complete incomplete images and fill in blank spaces. You might think of this as "jumping to conclusions." This is because people are generally not comfortable with things that are unfinished. On the other hand, creative people are less bothered by lack of completion.

WHAT TO LOOK FOR:

Compare the self-ratings with the perception test responses.

- Did the subjects who rated themselves as highly creative more often describe the figures as incomplete?
- Did the subjects who rated themselves as highly observant more often describe the figures as they really are?

Tip: If creative people are more comfortable with unfinished things, we might assume that they would see the figures as incomplete. We might also assume that less creative people would feel the need to label the figures. But neither assumption is necessarily true.

Section B, Part One:

1. A square of O's and a square of X's.

You might relate this to the way we often assume that all members of a group (racial, political, economic, etc.) are alike.

Section B, Part Two:

1. Columns of X's.

2. 4 groups.

People typically group things together when the things are alike or when they are near to one another. You might relate this to the way we judge people as being like the people they hang around with (guilt by association?), or the way we assume that because people are together, they must be alike.

Section C:

1. A football.

Most people will see the football shape because the natural tendency is to see the figure that includes the greatest number of elements in any design. We prefer a neat, tidy package with no "left-overs."

WHAT TO LOOK FOR:

- Did the subjects who rated themselves as highly social see these typical groupings more often than those who rated themselves as less social?
- Were the subjects who rated themselves as highly organized more or less likely to see the typical groupings?

CONCLUSIONS

- Did most of your subjects give the typical responses to the Visual Perception Test?

EXPLORE MORE

- Repeat this experiment with left-handed people and right-handed people. Are their perceptions similar or different? Try it with males and females, young people and elderly people, tall people and short people, teachers and students. What conclusions can you draw?
- Use the illusions on page 55 to make up more experiments in perception. Copy them, cut them apart, and show them one at a time. *Examples:* How long does it take each subject to figure out each visual illusion? How quickly can they draw the impossible magnet? Is it easier to see the dog in the woods from close up or farther away? Is it easier to see the "E" if they have already been shown the "ABC"? (If so, they may be thinking "letters.")

Key to the Illusions

A. The letter E

B. A man on horseback

C. A dog in the woods

D. A white question mark on a black background, or a black bird with its wings outspread

E. The letters A, B, C

F. An impossible magnet...look closely!

WHY IT MATTERS TO YOU

- The rules of perception tell you a lot about the way the brain organizes the world. Since you naturally group things together when they look alike, you must be extra careful not to do the same with people. Remind yourself that when you group people together, you lose sight of their individual qualities.
- We tend to see things that are close together as being alike. Be careful not to see people this way. If you believe that people automatically think or act alike just because they happen to be in the same country, neighborhood, school, or family, you may miss opportunities to know people you would really like to know.
- In Section A of the Visual Perception Test, most subjects were probably ready to see the circle and square, even though these figures are incomplete in the illustration. This is something else to avoid in our relationships—filling in missing information and jumping to conclusions that aren't supported by facts.
- If you feel like you stand out in a crowd, or if you're self-conscious about people looking at you when you're in a group, just remember that the natural way of seeing is to see things—and people—as groups. It's very unlikely that people are noticing you in particular when you're surrounded by others.

DID YOU KNOW?

These "Rules of Seeing" can help you to improve your drawing skills:

- Distant objects appear smaller, dimmer, and fuzzier.
- Nearby objects appear larger, clearer, and brighter.
- Nearer objects overlap and cover objects behind them if they are in the same line of vision.
- In a two-dimensional field, the nearer objects appear at the bottom and the distant objects at the top.
- When you are riding in a car, near objects seem to pass by more rapidly than those at a moderate distance. Objects at a very far distance, like the moon, seem to be following you.

VISUAL PERCEPTION TEST

SECTION A: THE LAW OF COMPLETION

1. What do you see here?

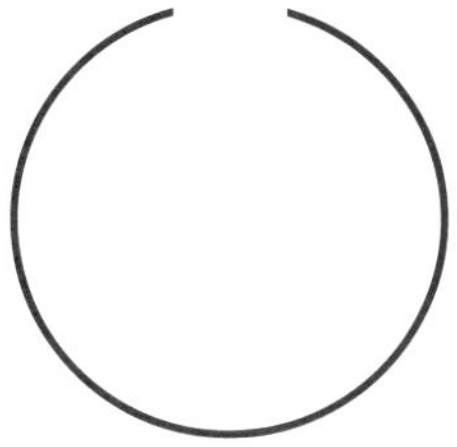

2. What do you see here?

3. What do you see here?

4. How many triangles?

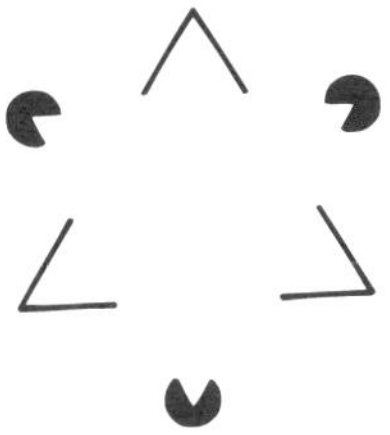

SECTION B: LAWS OF GROUPING

Part One: Similarity

1. Is this two squares of O's and one square of X's, or two horizontal rows of O's and X's mixed?

O O X X O O
O O X X O O

Part Two: Nearness

1. Are these columns of X's or rows (across) of double X's?

XX XX XX
XX XX XX
XX XX XX
XX XX XX

2. How many groups of dots are there?

SECTION C: LAW OF INCLUSION

1. Is this a football, a square with two leftovers, or two triangles?

____
Signature

HOW DO YOU RATE YOURSELF?

Read each question, then circle the number that you think best describes you.

0 = low

3 = average

5 = high

How creative are you?	**0**	**1**	**2**	**3**	**4**	**5**

How observant are you?	**0**	**1**	**2**	**3**	**4**	**5**

How social are you?	**0**	**1**	**2**	**3**	**4**	**5**

How organized are you?	**0**	**1**	**2**	**3**	**4**	**5**

____

Signature

A

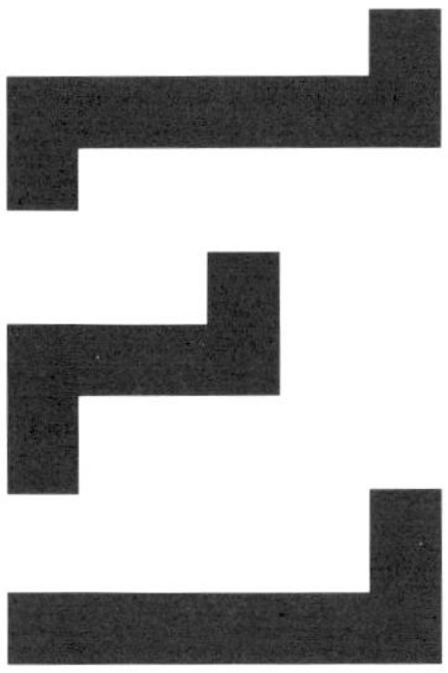

B

C

D

E

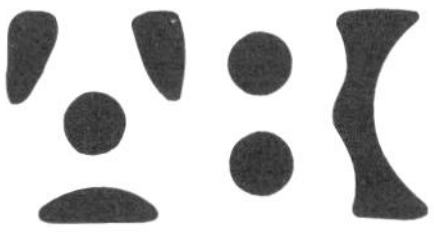

F

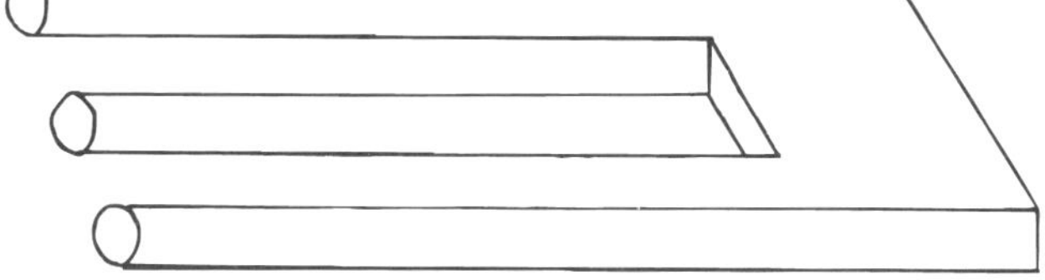

Does Caffeine Influence People's Perceptions?

What do drugs do to our perceptions? This experiment examines one effect of a drug most people consider harmless and use every day.

SUBJECTS

- As many people as you want to test who already use caffeine (in coffee, tea, cocoa, or cola)

WHAT YOU NEED

- A copy of the cube picture on page 58
- A timer or clock with second hand
- Drinks containing caffeine (cola, coffee, tea, cocoa), one for each subject
- Paper and pencil for tallying responses; list each subject's name, then label two columns "Before Caffeine" and "After Caffeine"
- Paper and pencil for recording observations and results, or a copy of the Experiment Data Sheet on page 7

WHAT TO DO

Repeat all 4 steps for each subject. You may want to complete steps 1 and 2 first for all subjects, then do steps 3 and 4 for all subjects.

1. Have your subject look at the cube picture. Say, "You'll notice that the picture seems to flip every few seconds. The A corner looks nearer and the B corner farther away, then B looks nearer and A farther away. You're either looking down at the box or up at it."
2. Tell your subject to signal you whenever he or she sees the cube flip. Time your subject for one minute. Record the number of times your subject signals you.
3. Have your subject drink a cup of coffee, tea, cocoa, or cola with caffeine.
4. Wait 15 minutes, then repeat steps 1 and 2.

CONCLUSIONS

- Do subjects see more flips before or after caffeine? (They are likely to see more *after* caffeine, because caffeine is a drug that speeds up perception.)

EXPLORE MORE

- How could speeded-up perception influence the way you function during specific tasks like reading, writing, studying, listening to music, driving, talking, and listening to other people talk?
- Take an informal survey to find out how many of your friends use caffeine. Find out how much they use on average each day. Do they sometimes have trouble sleeping? Do they feel tense, edgy, jittery, anxious, stressed-out, headachy, irritable? These are all signs that they are using too much caffeine.

WHY IT MATTERS TO YOU

- Your diet (what you eat and drink) not only influences your physical and mental health and mood. It also affects the way you see the world. When you add this to the many other things that influence your perceptions, it's easy to understand why no two people see things in exactly the same way.

DID YOU KNOW?

- Caffeine is a mild poison. A fatal daily dose for humans is 60–100 cups.
- It's possible to get hooked on caffeine by consuming as little as 200–400 milligrams per day—4 cans of regular cola or 4 cups of coffee.

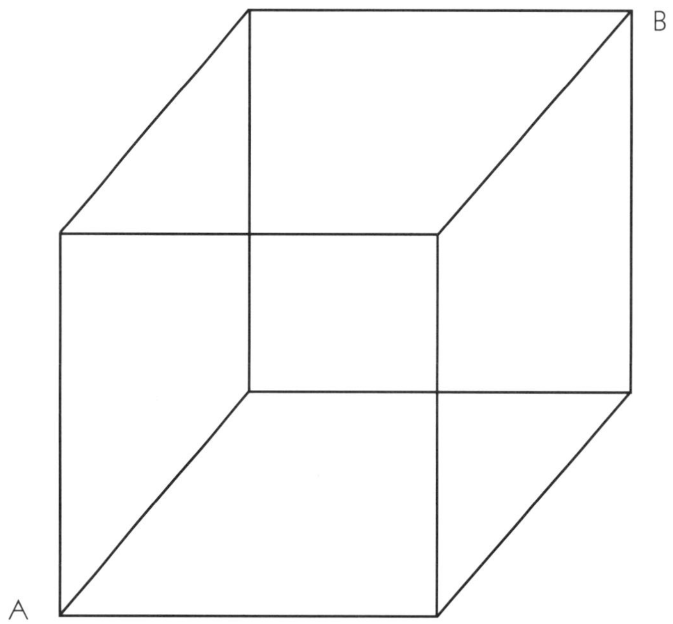
B
A

How Much Personal Space Do People Need?

When you think about space exploration, you probably don't think about the kind of space you will explore in this experiment. Although your discoveries won't make the evening news, they can be important to your understanding and tolerance of other people.

SUBJECTS

- You and the people in a public place—a store or shopping mall, library, school cafeteria, school grounds, etc.

WHAT YOU NEED

- Paper and pencil for recording observations and results, or a copy of the Experiment Data Sheet on page 7

WHAT TO DO

1. Pretend you are doing whatever is expected in the public place you choose to try your experiment. *Example:* If you choose a shopping mall, act as if you are shopping.
2. Slowly and gradually, move closer and closer to another person. Don't get so near that you look obvious or make the other person upset or angry.
3. Make a mental note of the person's reaction. At what point does he or she seem to feel uncomfortable and move away? Does the person move away in order to maintain a certain distance between you?

CONCLUSIONS

- Have you ever felt uncomfortable when someone moved too close to you in a public place? Maybe you were at the video store and another person wanted to look at the same shelf you were standing in front of. To make you move away, the person came into your personal space.
- Different cultures develop different rules for personal space. Do you have any theories about why this happens?

EXPLORE MORE

- If you're a female, have a male friend try this experiment. If you're a male, have a female friend try it. See if your friend gets the same reactions you did, or if people react differently. Can you draw any conclusions?
- Close your eyes. Have someone hold his or her hand about one foot above your arm and very gradually come closer. When you "feel" that the hand is 1/2" away, say "Stop." Open your eyes. What do you find? What does this tell you about where your skin "stops"?
- Do a schoolwide experiment on personal space. Have pairs of students stand about 6 feet apart from each other, then gradually draw closer together. Who feels uncomfortable first? Does it matter if the students are from the same cultural background? What happens when you mix people from different cultural backgrounds? Following your experiment, analyze your data. Can you draw any conclusions? What does this experiment show about cultural differences, diversity, and tolerance?
- Talk to people from cultural backgrounds different from your own. Compare family rules and customs. List things your families always or never do. *Examples:* Some families expect people to remove their shoes when they enter their homes. Some allow their pets to lick the leftovers from the dishes after dinner. Some wash canned goods when they bring them home from the store. Some wash bananas before they eat them. Do any of these rules or customs seem normal to you? Do any seem unusual? If you can't find people from different cultural backgrounds, then compare your family rules and customs with those of your friends' families.

WHY IT MATTERS TO YOU

- Sometimes people from different countries and cultures don't get along because their perceptions are basically different. They don't understand each others' perceptions or communicate their own very clearly. When you travel, or even when you visit someone else's home or neighborhood, you are entering another culture. Families, like cultures, have certain customs that you may not be aware of. When people do things that seem rude, thoughtless, or strange to you, try to be understanding. Their actions may be perfectly acceptable and normal within their own culture. Remember that you might be doing things they consider rude, thoughtless, or strange. Who is to say who's right about customs?

DID YOU KNOW?

- Different cultural perceptions and expectations can lead to awkward situations. *Example:* An American family wasn't happy with the behavior of a foreign exchange student who was staying with them. They didn't want to come right out and tell him, so they tried to communicate their dissatisfaction by giving him the silent treatment. They weren't aware that in the student's culture, people often become quiet to signal that they want to be alone. The student figured that the Americans just wanted to be alone. He didn't know anything was wrong until the family took him into town and put him on a bus!

Can We Tell the Difference between Male and Female Touch?

With a simple handshake or a tap on the shoulder, touch can tell you a lot about how someone feels about you and about himself or herself. This experiment explores whether a touch can reveal someone's identity—or at least his or her gender.

SUBJECTS

- 1 person

WHAT YOU NEED

- A blindfold
- An equal number of male and female assistants
- A carpeted room (or have assistants remove their shoes)
- A chair for your subject
- Paper and pencil for tallying responses; write your subject's name at the top, list each assistant's name, then label two columns "Right" and "Wrong"
- Paper and pencil for recording observations and results, or a copy of the Experiment Data Sheet on page 7

WHAT TO DO

1. Have your subject sit in the chair. Blindfold your subject. Say, "Several people will enter the room and touch your forehead, one at a time. Try to identify each person's gender. When you think you know, say 'Male' or 'Female.'"
2. Have your assistants enter the room without speaking and stand quietly behind the blindfolded subject.
3. Have each assistant approach your subject and touch his or her forehead for 3 seconds, using only a forefinger. The assistants should be as quiet as possible so they don't give any clues to their identities.
4. As your subject says "Male" or "Female," record responses as "right" or "wrong" (or have an assistant record them). Don't let your subject know if a response was right or wrong until the end of the experiment.

CONCLUSIONS

- How successful was your subject at identifying the genders of the touchers?
- Ask your subject, "On what did you base your decisions?" Possible clues include skin temperature, the amount of pressure in the touch, evidence of perfume or other scent, long or short fingernails, the person's overall presence, etc.
- What are some other ways your subject might have identified the touchers?

EXPLORE MORE

- If your blindfolded subject was a female, repeat the experiment with a male subject. Compare results. Can you draw any conclusions? Repeat your experiment with several female and male subjects. Does it seem that males and females are equally good at guessing, or does one gender seem better than the other at guessing?
- Repeat the experiment with assistants who are friends of your subject (or, if you used friends in your original experiment, try it with people who are strangers to your subject). Would you expect it to be easier for your subject to identify the touch of a stranger or of a friend?
- Try wearing a piece of jewelry where you don't usually wear one. *Examples:* a bracelet on your left hand (if you usually wear one on your right hand or not at all), a ring on your middle finger (if you usually wear one on your ring finger or not at all), etc. See how long it takes before you no longer feel it touching your skin. Your reaction/response to anything gets weaker when you are exposed to it for long periods of time. You get used to it. Eventually it will seem as if the piece of jewelry isn't even there.

  In a somewhat similar way, society may get used to (stop noticing) things like pollution and violence. Individuals may stop noticing and appreciating loved ones. Can you think of other examples of this phenomenon?
- How is getting used to something useful, and how is it harmful? List some things you have gotten used to. *Examples:* Maybe you have to roll down the car window to open the door from the outside because the handle on the inside doesn't work. Although this was extremely annoying at first, you may have gotten used to it. Or you may not even notice that you have to tap the top of your dresser to make a broken drawer open. But when a visitor asks, "Why are you doing that?," you suddenly notice how you have gotten used to the broken drawer.

WHY IT MATTERS TO YOU

- When you learn that people have different levels of sensitivity—not only for touch but also for noise, brightness, confusion, and other things—you can become more tolerant of what may seem like unreasonable expectations or behaviors. Often people are not really trying to be annoying. They just experience their surroundings in different ways and have different needs.

DID YOU KNOW?

- Some people claim to be so sensitive to touch that they can "feel" colors when they are blindfolded. You can test this by having a red ball, a yellow notebook, a blue pen, a white paper bag, and a green piece of paper in a cardboard box in a dark room. Have a blindfolded subject try to identify the colors by touch alone. Can you find anyone with this ability? (It isn't likely.)
- There is a rare condition in which people's senses "cross over" so the people really do "taste" shapes, "feel" colors, etc. This is not a psychological problem or an overactive imagination. It's an actual neurological condition called *synesthesia*.

COMMUNICATION

Do the Words People Use Reveal Their Personalities?

Based on the language someone speaks, you might be able to tell what part of the world he or she is from. Based on the accent, you might even be able to identify the region. But can you tell anything about how people think or feel from the words they use? This experiment takes a look at the relationship between words and personality.

SUBJECTS

- Any number of adults

WHAT YOU NEED

- Copies of the Sentences Exercise on page 67, one for each subject
- Copies of the Questionnaire on page 68, one for each subject
- Paper and pencils for your subjects
- Paper and pencil for recording observations and results, or a copy of the Experiment Data Sheet on page 7

WHAT TO DO

1. Have each subject complete and sign the Sentences Exercise. Notice that the words on the word list can be read either as action words or as words that name or describe something.
2. Next, have each subject complete and sign the Questionnaire. It's important to give the Questionnaire *after* your subjects have completed the Sentences Exercise. Otherwise the "first impression" effect might take over, and their sentences will be shaped by their answers about their preferences.

Scoring the Activities

SENTENCES EXERCISE

Add up the number of times subjects perceived the words as verbs.

- 0–5 = less action-oriented
- 6–10 = more action-oriented

QUESTIONNAIRE

- Question #1: Give 2 points for a physical activity (swimming, skiing, running), 0 points for a more quiet activity (reading, drawing, cooking).
- Question #2: Give 2 points for a physical activity (camping, hiking), 0 points for a more quiet activity (fishing, sunbathing).
- Question #3: Give 1 point each for a and c, 0 points each for b and d.
- Question #4: Give 2 points for a, 0 points for b.
- Question #5: Give 2 points for a verb, 0 points for a noun.

Add up the points from the Questionnaire:

- Total possible points = 12
- 0–6 points = less active
- 7–12 points = more active

CONCLUSIONS

- For each subject, compare the scores for the two activities in this experiment. Start by looking at the Questionnaire score. Is your subject more active or less active? Then look at the Sentences Exercise score. Are the scores consistent?
- Do more active people see the words in the Sentences Exercise as verbs?
- Do less active people see the words in the Sentences Exercise as nouns or adjective?

EXPLORE MORE

- Use the Sentences Exercise and Questionnaire to compare male and female responses.
- Think of a situation that makes you mad: "______________ MAKES ME MAD." How much of your anger comes from the fact that you don't have control over that situation?
- Think again about the phrase, "_______ MAKES ME MAD." Does the language itself suggest that something or someone is forcing you to be angry—that you have no choice about how to feel? When something MAKES you mad, it has power over your feelings. But what if you say, "I CHOOSE to be mad"? With this language, you take back some control of and responsibility for your feelings. You will probably discover that you feel *less* angry when you use this language. The same is true for fear.

WHY IT MATTERS TO YOU

- Your writing and speech will be easier to understand and more lively if you remember to use active language rather than passive language. *Examples:* "I hit the ball" sounds better than "The ball was hit by me." Active language also gives the impression that you are more confident and in control of the situation. It may even make you feel more self-assured. Either way, your use of active or passive language tells other people something about you.
- Words and phrases that can be understood in more than one way are called "ambiguous language." If someone speaks to you in ambiguous language, you are forced to fill in a meaning for what he or she is saying. Because you tend to choose a meaning closely related to your own experience, you may assume that the person really "knows" you or is very "intuitive." This is why some people may hit it off when they first meet each other, only to find out later that they have very little in common.
- Teenagers often speak a language that adults are not supposed to understand. This language has a very specific purpose: It helps young people to define who they are and how they are different from their parents' generation. They use their special language to become more independent. What are some words you use that your parents might not be familiar with?

DID YOU KNOW?

- Today there are 2,796 languages spoken in the world. A few centuries ago, there were more than 10,000. The last surviving speaker of an unidentified Native American tribe died in California before scientists were able to make a tape recording of his language. Imagine being the only person who speaks your language. What would you read? What would you do? How would your life be different?
- Language is not just communication. It's also a diagram of very basic ways people think about time, space, and relationships. You can learn a lot about other cultures if you study the way they use language. *Example:* In the Hopi language, you would not speak of a "hot summer" because "summer" is the condition of being hot. Language differences often make it difficult to communicate in a foreign language, even if you have studied it for many years and know it very well.
- *Was ist das?* The Continental Congress once considered adopting German as the official language of the United States. English won by only one vote. How might history be different if the German language had won?

SENTENCES EXERCISE

Please write a sentence using each of the following words:

1. PEAKED

____

2. ATTRIBUTE

____

3. WIND

____

4. RACE

____

5. PRESENT

____

6. QUESTION

____

7. CHECK

____

8. OBJECT

____

9. INSULT

____

10. LIVE

____

____
Signature

QUESTIONNAIRE

1. Name one of your hobbies or interests: ______________________________
____

2. Describe one thing you like to do on vacation: ______________________
____

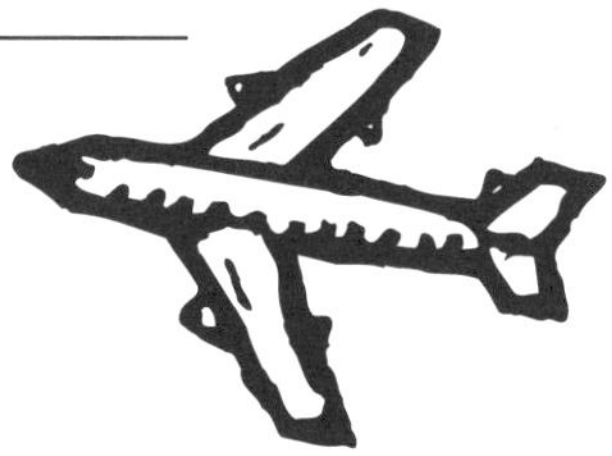

3. Which two of the following activities would you prefer to do?

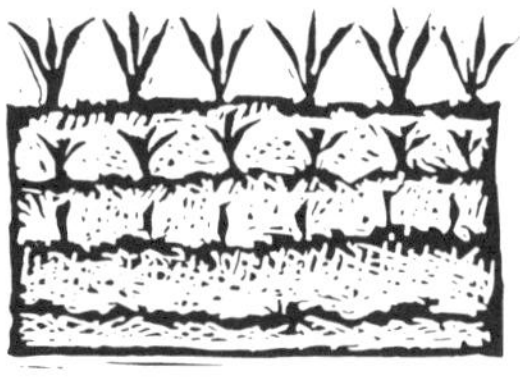

___ a. work in the garden

___ b. watch television

___ c. jog or take a walk

___ d. go to a play or movie

4. Would you rather play a sport or watch a sport?

___ a. play

___ b. watch

5. Write one noun or one verb that you feel describes you: ______________

____
Signature

Can We Listen to Our Parents as People?

Sometimes things your parents say sound different to you than they would if someone else said them. You might hear your parents' words as "hidden advice" or as an attempt to control you. Don't worry; this is perfectly natural! This experiment gives you a chance to try something new. It is a self-observation.

SUBJECTS

- You and your parents

WHAT YOU NEED

- Paper and pencil for recording observations and results, or a copy of the Experiment Data Sheet on page 7

WHAT TO DO

1. For one week or one month, make a real effort to hear your parents as if they are people who just happen to know you. *Example:* The words "You should..." coming from a parent are usually heard as a command or a criticism of something you are already doing. "You should do this..." can sound like "You should *not* do what you are doing." During the experiment, try hearing "You should..." the way you would hear a friend say it—as "It might be interesting to try..." or "You might want to think about...." Often, when your parents say "You should...," this is exactly what they mean, too.
2. As you do this experiment, keep notes about your feelings and about how communication between you and your parents changes, if it does.

CONCLUSIONS

- After the experiment, discuss it with your parents. Explain what you were trying to learn and what you discovered along the way. Can you think of any situations that turned out differently than they might have because you listened differently than you used to?
- How might this experiment relate to Experiment #1, "Do People Get What They Expect?"
- How do the labels "parent" and "child" affect the way we talk to and hear one another?
- Would you recommend this experiment as a way to better understand your parents as people?

EXPLORE MORE

- See if your parents will agree to try a different version of this experiment. Can they listen to what *you* say as if you're just another person and not their child? Can they do this for a week or a month?
- See if you can tell who other members of your family are talking to on the phone by listening to the way they talk. You'll probably be able to guess whether the other person is someone they know well or someone they don't know at all. You might be able to get more specific and identify the person on the other end.

  You'll be amazed by how much you can tell from someone's tone of voice. Think of a time when you were expecting a call, picked up the phone, and said "Hi" in a certain way. When you discovered that the caller wasn't the person you were expecting, your tone of voice changed.

WHY IT MATTERS TO YOU

- If this experiment improved your relationship with your parents, you might want to try it again, this time for 20 years!

DID YOU KNOW?

- Often, relationships and communication are influenced by the labels we put on people. *Examples:* We might talk very loudly to someone who is visually impaired, as if not being able to see well reduces one's ability to hear. Or we might use a special tone of voice when talking to small children and elderly persons. Nurses may use the word "we" when talking to patients, as in "How are we feeling today?"
- The word "parent" describes a relationship; the word "child" describes a relationship and an age range. There is no commonly used English word for a grown-up child. Some people use "adult children," but this sounds odd. Words such as "offspring" and "progeny" describe a relationship, but we don't use them very often. Why do you think the English language seems to be missing such an important word? Does this word exist in any other languages? Try to find out.

Is One Way of Communicating Better Than Another?

This experiment tests two different ways for the people in a group to communicate and relate. Tell your subjects that you're going to do an experiment, but to make it more fun, you're going to treat it as a game.

SUBJECTS

- 10 people divided into 2 groups of 5 people each (Company W and Company C)

WHAT YOU NEED

- 2 copies of Communication Styles on page 74, one for each group
- 2 copies of the Word Lists on page 75, each cut into 5 individual lists 1, 2, 3, 4, and 5 (you should have 10 separate lists in all)
- 10 copies of the Logic Puzzle on page 76, one for each subject
- A timer or clock with second hand
- Paper, pencils, and scissors for your subjects
- Paper and pencil for recording observations and results, or a copy of the Experiment Data Sheet on page 7

WHAT TO DO

1. Introduce the experiment by saying, "Company W and Company C are competitors. Each is developing a new video game. The company that is first to solve two important problems—a word problem and a logic problem—will be the first to get its product on the market, while the other company will go broke.

   "Company W is organized as a wheel, with a boss in the middle of the circle. The employees can communicate *only* with the boss." Choose someone to be the boss or ask for a volunteer.

   Continue by saying, "Company C is organized as a circle. Every employee can communicate with the person on either side of him or her."

   Give each group a copy of Communication Styles. Have the groups rearrange their chairs to look like the illustrations.

2. Say, "Your first problem is to find the password you need to open your new video game. It was lost in the computer and nobody remembers it. The only way to find the password is by comparing several word lists and finding one word that appears on all of the lists. That is your password."

3. Give each subject in Company W one word list—1, 2, 3, 4, or 5. Do the same for Company C. Then say, "Study your word lists and try to figure out which word appears on all of the lists. Company W, because your company is organized as a wheel, you can communicate *only* with your boss. Company C, because your company is organized as a circle, you can communicate *only* with the person on either side of you."

   Make sure that everyone understands who they can and can't communicate with. Instruct them to speak very quietly so they can't be overheard by the people they aren't supposed to be communicating with. Tell each group to raise their hands when they have solved the problem. Time each group. (The common word is "squeak.")

4. After both groups have solved the word problem, say, "Company W is now under new management. They have decided to use the circle arrangement to communicate. Meanwhile, Company C has switched to the wheel communication style." Have the two groups rearrange their chairs to match their new communication styles. Choose someone to be the boss of Company C or ask for a volunteer. Remind Company W that they now have no boss.

5. Say, "Your second problem is to create a display sign for your new video game. To do this, you will need to solve a logic problem."

Give each subject in both groups a copy of the Logic Puzzle, a piece of paper, a pencil, and scissors.

Make sure that everyone understands who they can and can't communicate with. Remind them to speak very quietly. Tell each group to raise their hands when they have solved the problem. Time each group.

? CONCLUSIONS

- Which group solved the word problem faster, Company W (wheel) or Company C (circle)? Is this what you expected?
- Which group solved the logic puzzle faster, Company W (communicating as a circle) or Company C (communicating as a wheel)? Is this what you expected?

Solution to Logic Puzzle

1. Crease the paper lengthwise and reopen.

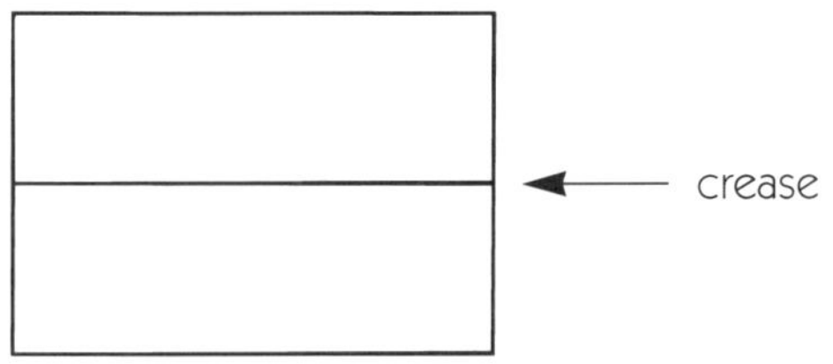

2. Cut on dotted lines.

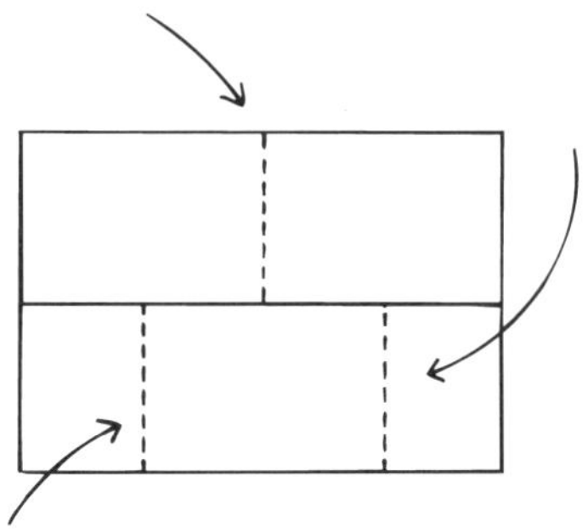

3. Flip the shaded section forward 180 degrees.

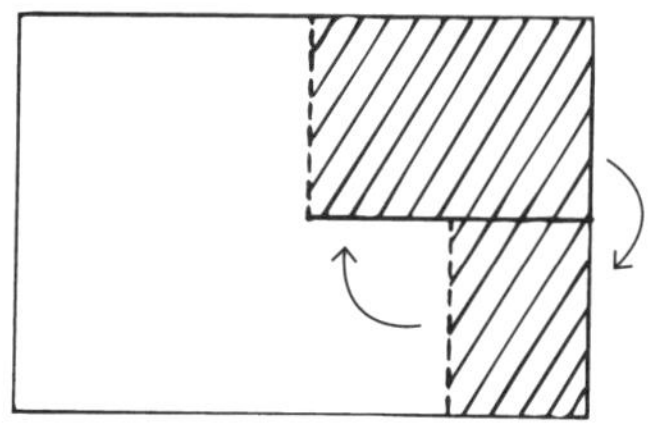

The sign should stand on its own.

P.S. You can also make this stand-up sign without making the crease, if you cut carefully. Once you do this, the puzzle is even more mysterious. Try it on your friends.

EXPLORE MORE

- Discuss with both groups what they think of each method of communication. Make a list, with their help, of the advantages and disadvantages of each way of communicating.
- Think of other possible ways of communicating that might work well. Repeat this experiment to test your new ideas.

WHY IT MATTERS TO YOU

- You can see that it's important to have some sort of organized way for people in a group to collect their thoughts. By experimenting with different ways to communicate with others, you'll find even better ways to work together.

DID YOU KNOW?

- The best way to work with others may depend on the situation. *Example:* In an emergency, when there is no time for everyone to talk, listen, and agree on a solution, it's often smartest and most effective for one person to take charge and tell everyone else what to do.
- In most other situations, solving problems is easier and faster when everyone can get feedback about what's going right and what's going wrong. Which communication type gives more feedback, the wheel or the circle?

COMMUNICATION STYLES

COMPANY W: WHEEL

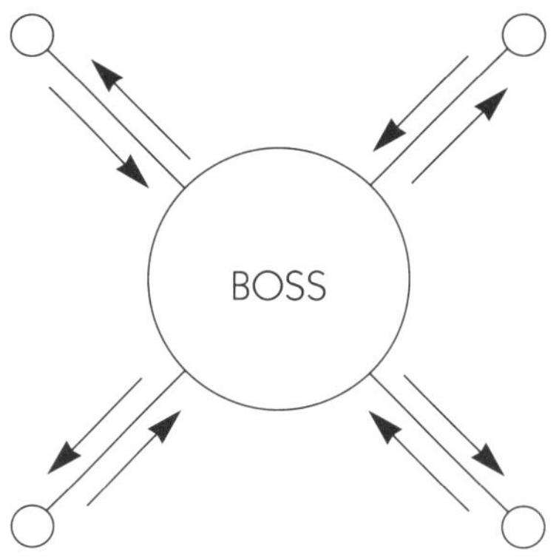

You can communicate only with your boss.

COMPANY C: CIRCLE

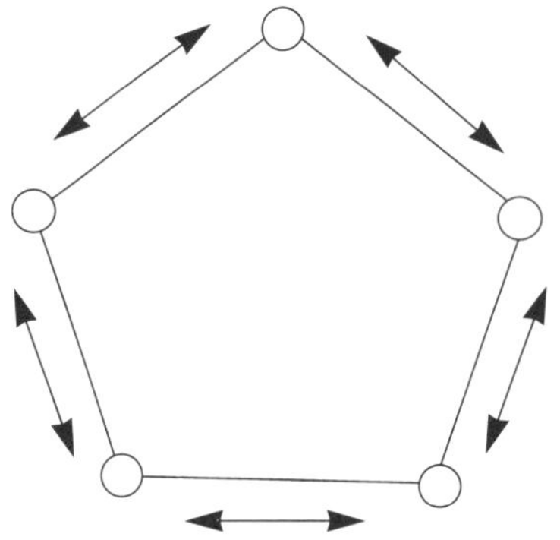

You can communicate only with the person on either side of you.

WORD LISTS

LIST 1	LIST 2	LIST 3	LIST 4	LIST 5
ANGLE	MONEY	PUNCH	SQUEAK	MOUSE
LUNCH	FISH	PAGE	TIME	TILE
MODERN	HAPPY	APPLE	WEST	FINAL
WORN	SQUEAK	ZERO	EMPTY	CRATER
SUN	COAT	TOP	ROPE	SQUEAK
BROKEN	CHAIN	YO-YO	PENCIL	TREE
FOLDER	WIDE	SQUARE	GOLD	NOSE
SQUEAK	CARPET	EAGLE	COW	TAPE
PLANE	FLOWER	BLUE	GROUND	BROWN
WRITE	RADIO	SQUEAK	SHIRT	GRASS

LOGIC PUZZLE

Can you make this display sign using only 3 cuts and a fold?

FRONT VIEW

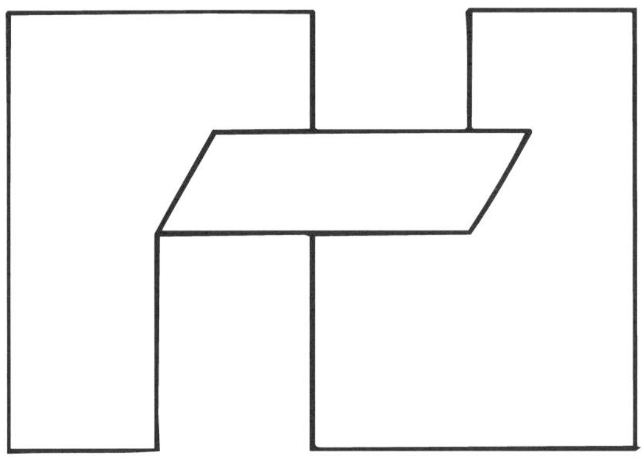

TOP VIEW

Why Ask Questions?

Clear, complete communication depends on many different things. This experiment explores the importance of feedback in good communication. It asks the question, "What happens when you can't ask a question?"

SUBJECTS

- You and a partner

WHAT YOU NEED

- 2 identical sets of blocks that are different shapes and colors (if you don't have these, just cut out triangles, squares, rectangles, and circles in green, blue, red, and yellow. Make a few of each color in each shape. The exact number isn't important as long as you have 2 identical sets)
- A notebook or playing board from a board game
- Paper and pencil for recording observations and results, or a copy of the Experiment Data Sheet on page 7

WHAT TO DO

1. Sit at a table—you on one side, your partner on the other side. Set up the notebook or playing board as a barrier. Keep one set of blocks or shapes and give the other set to your partner.

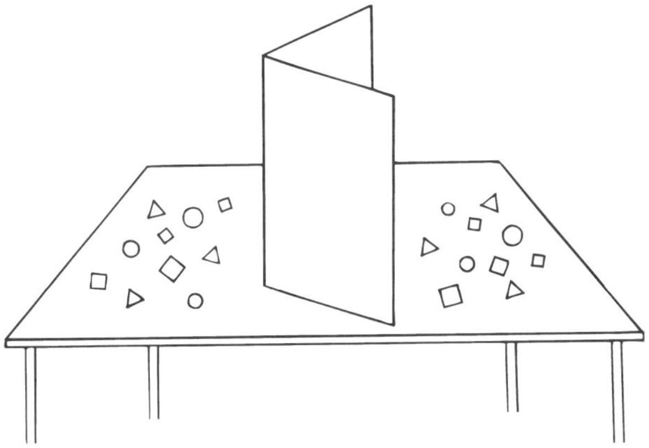

2. Working behind the barrier so your partner can't see what you are doing, build a 3-dimensional structure from the blocks or a flat design from the paper shapes.

   Now explain to your partner that you are in a spaceship circling the planet Zug—a friendly planet, but one whose residents know nothing about Earth technology. Your ship is in trouble and you must land, but before you can do so, the Zuggian air traffic controller (your partner) needs to understand what your instrument panel looks like. Luckily, you speak the same language, so you can describe your panel.

Unluckily, the Zuggian cannot respond or ask questions because the communication equipment on Zug is malfunctioning. Also, the Zuggian can't see you, so don't use any body language.

Your partner has an identical set of blocks or papers. As you describe your instrument panel, he or she should try to make an exact copy. Remember that your communication can only be one-way. Afterward, remove the barrier and see how close your partner came to re-creating your design.

Can you land on Zug?

CONCLUSIONS

- Is it possible to communicate clearly and completely when only one person can talk and the other isn't allowed to respond or ask questions?
- How important is it to be able to ask questions and have them answered?
- How important is body language to communication?

EXPLORE MORE

- Switch roles and repeat the experiment. What is it like to be told to do something without being able to ask questions?
- Repeat the experiment, only this time allow your partner to respond and ask questions.
- Is it easier to tell when someone is lying to you over the phone or in person? The answer may surprise you. Experiments have shown that it's easier to tell when someone is lying to you over the phone. When you listen to people without seeing them, you do a better job of really hearing what they are saying. Body language can often "charm" and distract a listener…but not over the phone. Find out for yourself. Give 2 of your friends a list of 12 questions to ask you. Have one friend interview you over the phone and the other in person. Answer half of the questions with lies. Which interviewer is able to guess which questions you lied about?

WHY IT MATTERS TO YOU

- There is no such thing as a dumb question. If you want to learn anything, you have to ask questions!
- Asking questions is what experimenting is all about.

DID YOU KNOW?

- 55% of the messages you send to others are in the form of body language. 38% are sent with your tone of voice. Only 7% of the messages you send to others are in words.
- Is it easier to tell when someone on the radio is lying, or when someone on television is lying? Experiments have shown that it's easier to tell when someone on the radio is lying. Compare this to the experiments about phone/in person lying (see "Explore More"). This should give you some clues about why television conceals and radio reveals a liar.
- Dogs have their own body language. Knowing the basics will make you less likely to be misunderstood or attacked by a strange dog. Here are some tips to keep in mind:
  - Don't smile. A strange dog may see it as a threat.
  - Don't stare directly at the dog. Staring tells the dog that *you* want to be Top Dog—it's a challenge.
  - Don't shout or raise your arms above your head. This will make the dog angry.
  - Any swiftly moving object might trigger a dog's chase instinct.
  - Act submissive. Hold your arms against your sides and try to look small.
  - Make chewing sounds. According to a Danish dog psychologist, mammals are calmed by the sounds of chewing.

Tips on Using Language in Positive Ways

1. Be more precise with words you use to describe your feelings. *Example:* Instead of saying that you "like" both Terry and Larry, it might be more accurate to say that you "respect" Terry and "appreciate" Larry.

2. When a friend wins something as a result of effort (like a speech contest or a race), don't say, "You're lucky!" This implies that your friend didn't really have to do anything to win. Instead, say, "You deserve it!" or "You earned it!"

3. When a friend accomplishes something (learning a new skill, performing in the school play), don't say, "I'm proud of you!" This implies that your friend did the work for your approval. Instead, you might say, "You must be proud of yourself!" That's what really matters.

4. Watch the language you use on yourself. When you make a mistake, don't tell yourself, "I failed." Instead, think about the experience and tell yourself, "I made a mistake, and this is what I learned from it...."

5. Avoid words like "frankly" or "to be honest" before making a statement. This implies that you're not frank or honest at other times.

6. When you tell someone that something is "right" or "wrong," the first thing they are likely to ask you is "Why?" In other words, to say a thing is "right" or "wrong" is simply not enough information to convince most people to listen to your advice.

   First, it's confusing because it's not clear what kind of "right" or "wrong" you are talking about. Suppose someone says to you, "It's wrong to say that Columbus discovered America." Does this mean that the information is wrong? Many people believe that Lief Ericson or other earlier explorers discovered America. Or does this mean that the statement is morally wrong? Many people believe that it's an insult to say that Columbus "discovered" America as if America (and the Native Americans) didn't exist until Columbus came to its shores. This is just one example of two very different ways the word "wrong" can be understood.

   Another problem is that insisting something is "wrong" may put up a communication barrier between you and the other person. Right away, you sound like a judge, and your listener may reach for earplugs. It's better for clear communication to use words such as "helpful" or "harmful," "useful" or "not useful."

   Compare these two statements:

   - "It's wrong to smoke."
   - "It's harmful to smoke."

   Which is more likely to be listened to? What two different attitudes do the two statements show? Which one shows caring? Which one shows judgment? Which contains more information? Which would you listen to?

7. Always try to state things as positively as you can. You'll get your point across more effectively than if you're negative or neutral. *Example:* Imagine that you're a waiter at a restaurant. A customer asks, "Can I order something that isn't on the menu?" You might say, "No, you can't" (negative), "I'll have to ask the chef" (neutral), or "I'll be glad to ask the chef for you" (positive). Which answer will please your customer more? A small change in language can make a big difference.

GENDER DIFFERENCES

Do Males and Females Have Different Thinking Styles?

Sometimes children argue that "girls are smarter than boys" or "boys are smarter than girls." In reality, we know that neither statement is true. There are some girls who are smarter than some boys, and some boys who are smarter than some girls. Research has shown that boys and girls, males and females may have different thinking styles. This experiment investigates that possibility.

SUBJECTS

- An equal number of males and females

WHAT YOU NEED

- Paper and pencils for your subjects
- Paper and pencil for recording observations and results, or a copy of the Experiment Data Sheet on page 7

WHAT TO DO

1. Ask your subjects to write "Male" or "Female" at the top of their paper. Then say, "Run through the alphabet in your head and count the number of letters with the long E sound, including the letter E. Don't count on your fingers. Write your answer on the left side of your paper and call it 'Task A.'" Give them a minute or two to finish this task.
2. Next, say, "Now imagine an alphabet of typed capital letters. Run through it in your head and count the number of letters that have one or more curves in them. Don't use your fingers. Write your answer on the right side of your paper and call it 'Task B.'" Give them a minute or two to finish this task.
3. When everyone has completed both tasks, give them the correct answers. (There are 9 long E sounds, 11 curved capital letters.)
4. Ask your subjects to answer these questions:
   - "Which task did you do better on, A or B?"
   - "Which task was easier for you?"
   - "How did you figure out the answer for each task? What was your thinking like?"

CONCLUSIONS

- In general, females make fewer errors on Task A and males make fewer errors on Task B.
- Task A is more auditory (related to hearing). Task B is more visual (related to seeing).
- If females in general really are better at auditory tasks, and males in general really are better at visual tasks, how might this affect their school performance? Choice of hobbies? Choice of careers?

EXPLORE MORE

- Sometimes, when people are in a group, they feel pressured when doing tasks like the ones in this experiment. Try this experiment with one person at a time and see if there is any change in the scores.

WHY IT MATTERS TO YOU

- When we say that males and females have different thinking styles, we are making a general statement that will not apply to every female and every male. Differences are interesting, but it's important to keep in mind that we are all more alike than we are different.
- Try the experiment on yourself. If you score high as an auditory learner, play to your strength by studying in ways that involve hearing and listening. *Examples:* Study with a friend; tape record something you need to learn and play it back; pay special attention to listening in class. If you score high as a visual learner, try studying in ways that involve seeing and looking. *Examples:* Pay special attention to the diagrams and illustrations in your books; draw something you need to learn; read everything your teachers write on the board.

DID YOU KNOW?

- Males often have a left foot and/or hand that is larger than the right. Females often have a right foot and/or hand that is larger than the left.
- According to popular beliefs, males spend more time girl-watching than females do boy-watching, and females are more likely to tie up the phone lines than males. Do the results of this experiment support these beliefs?

How Much Do People Know about Their Own Gender?

This is the first of two guest experiments in *Psychology for Kids II.* The original experiment includes a lot more detail and background, as well as statistical results and analysis. It was contributed by Malia C. Novak and Lisa L. Rybak, psychology students of teacher Jim Matiya at Carl Sandburg High School in Orland Park, Illinois.

SUBJECTS

- An equal number of males and females

WHAT YOU NEED

- Copies of Gender Differences on page 86, one for each subject
- Pencils for your subjects
- Paper and pencil for recording observations and results, or a copy of the Experiment Data Sheet on page 7

WHAT TO DO

1. Have your subjects complete and sign the Gender Differences test.
2. Score the tests to find out how much your subjects know about their own gender and the opposite gender.

Scoring the Test

ANSWERS:

- Men: 1, 2, 5, 7, 8, 9, 10
- Women: 3, 4, 6

HOW TO SCORE THE TEST:

- 0–3 correct: Subject knows very little about gender differences
- 4–7 correct: Subject knows more than the average person about gender differences
- 8–10 correct: Subject is an expert on gender differences

CONCLUSIONS

- Who scored higher on the test, males or females? Is this what you expected?

EXPLORE MORE

- Notice the reactions of the people taking the test. How do they react to their scores? How do they react to what they have learned?
- Use this book, the first *Psychology for Kids* book, or other psychology books to make up similar tests about psychological rather than physical differences.

WHY IT MATTERS TO YOU

- The more facts you know about the physiology and psychology of males and females, the more you will understand about your own gender and the opposite gender.

DID YOU KNOW?

- People believe that they know more about gender differences than they really do. They accept common knowledge and stereotypes without checking them out or learning the facts.
- At birth, most boys are larger than most girls. They have larger hearts, lungs, and brains.
- At birth, most girls are more mature than boys, with a more highly developed nervous system. They also have a faster heartbeat.
- Female infants are more interested in colors; male infants are more interested in patterns.
- A gene that causes the index finger to be shorter than the ring finger is dominant in males, so more males have this trait. (You can turn this into another experiment.)

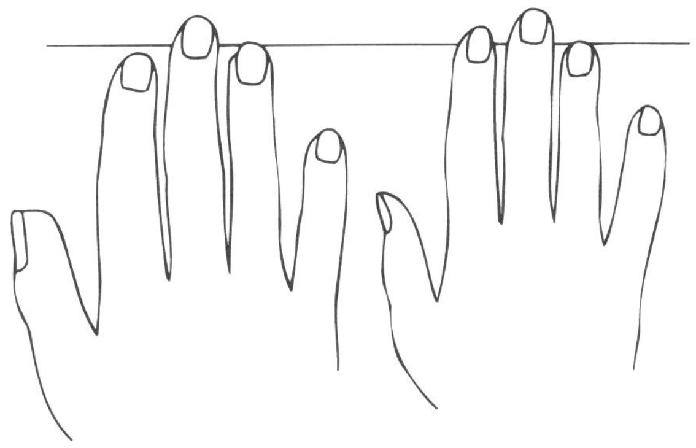

male hand female hand

GENDER DIFFERENCES

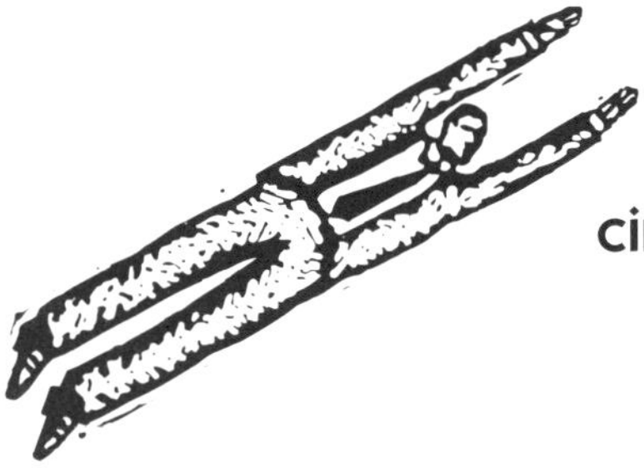

For each of the following questions, circle "M" if you think the answer is "Males," "F" if you think the answer is "Females."

1. Who sleepwalks more?	M	F
2. Whose eyes can't see the color red?	M	F
3. Whose forehead is more likely to feel warm?	M	F
4. Whose brain will recover faster from a stroke?	M	F
5. Who is more likely to hiccup?	M	F
6. Whose thumb is more likely to ache when it rains?	M	F
7. Who's that complaining of a painful toe?	M	F
8. Who's that gasping for air in the bedroom?	M	F
9. Who's most likely to wake up in the middle of the night with a pain in the gut?	M	F
10. Who has more red blood cells?	M	F

YOU ARE A (CIRCLE ONE) M F

____

Signature

Do We Picture Males and Females Differently?

Is it more or less likely that a picture of a head in a book or magazine will be a male? Is it more or less likely that a picture showing a whole person will be a female? This experiment explores those questions and some possible meanings for the answers.

SUBJECTS

- A group of people similar in age and background, with equal numbers of males and females

WHAT YOU NEED

- A copy of Which Is Male? Which Is Female? on page 89
- Paper and pencil for recording observations and results, or a copy of the Experiment Data Sheet on page 7

WHAT TO DO

1. Show your subjects the Which Is Male? Which Is Female? pictures.
2. Tell them that one is a male and the other is a female. Ask them which is which and how they know.

CONCLUSIONS

- Did most people say that the face with the body was female and the face without a body was male? What reasons did they give for their answers?
- Did all males give the same answers? Did all females give the same answers? If not, what were the differences?

EXPLORE MORE

- Look through magazines and newspapers for pictures of males and females. Are males usually pictured without bodies? Are females usually pictured with bodies? Researchers have found this to be true. Make your search more scientific by counting the actual numbers of male face/female face pictures and male body/female body pictures.

WHY IT MATTERS TO YOU

- It's good to be aware of how your culture perceives you and the groups you belong to, including gender. These perceptions can affect your life. If you know about them, you can work to change perceptions you believe to be wrong.

DID YOU KNOW?

- Researchers showed people two pictures of the same person: one of just the face, and one of the whole body. People rated the person "more intelligent" when they were shown the face photo. You might try a similar experiment.
- Researchers have found that photos of men in newspapers, magazines, ads, and news stories tend to emphasize their faces, while photos of women emphasize their bodies. About two-thirds of the average male photos show only the face, as compared to fewer than half of the average female photos. This same effect has been found in many different cultures around the world, as well as in paintings and drawings from the 17th through the 20th centuries.

Study the picture below. It looks a little strange, but not too bad. Turn it upside down and it's gruesome! Can you figure out what has been done to this picture? (You can turn this into another experiment.)

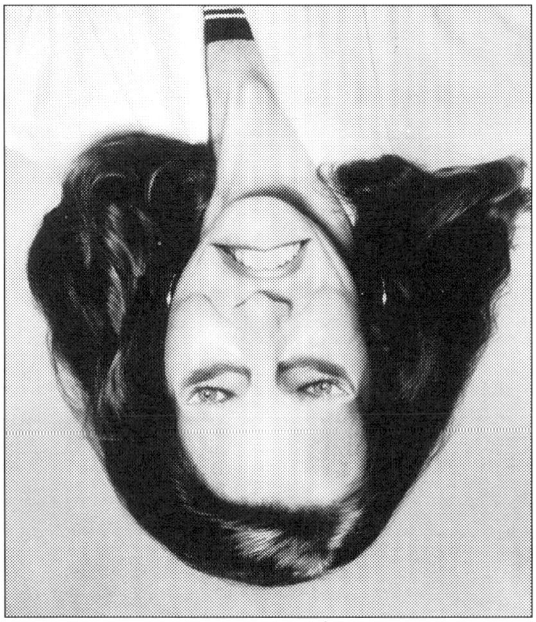

WHICH IS MALE? WHICH IS FEMALE?

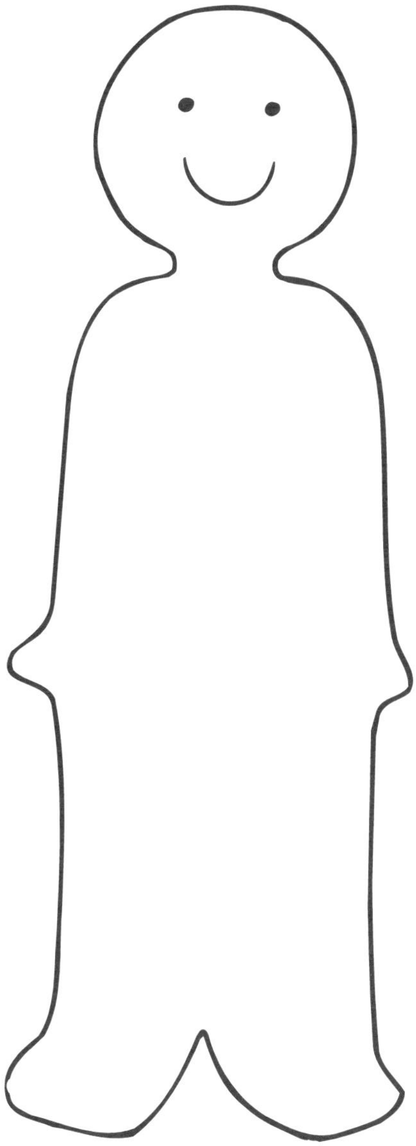

Do Males and Females See Things Differently?

Two or more people may look at the same thing, yet see it in completely different ways. *Example:* You're traveling with your family when you pull into a fast-food restaurant. The family member who is hungry sees it in one way, the family member who needs to use the restroom sees it in another way, and the child who notices the playground sees it in still another way. What we see depends on who we are and what we are most concerned with at that moment.

Does our gender have any influence on what we see? This experiment asks subjects to look at a picture that can be seen in more than one way, then define or describe it. Your task is to discover whether their view is related in some way to their gender.

SUBJECTS

- An equal number of males and females

WHAT YOU NEED

- Copies of What Is It? on page 93, one for each subject
- Pencils for your subjects
- Paper and pencil for recording observations and results, or a copy of the Experiment Data Sheet on page 7

WHAT TO DO

1. Give each subject a copy of What Is It? and have them write about what they think each picture looks like.
2. When they are finished, ask them to identify themselves as "Male" or "Female" at the top of the page.
3. Collect the papers, separate them into two piles (male and female), and record the responses.

Possibilities

Following are some responses given by people who have completed the What Is It? exercise:

1. butterfly, insect, leaves, plant, bow
2. snake, worm, string, ribbon, wiggle
3. moon, cookie with a bite out of it, pod
4. bat, bow tie, hair bow
5. match, needle, hairpin
6. spoon, dipper, baseball hat, snail
7. dunce cap, sailboat, pyramid, funnel, piece of pie, pizza slice, top
8. window, floor tile, package with a tie around it
9. spring, coil, telephone cord, ribbon, a bunch of "L's," 5 people
10. watch, band-aid, propeller, belt

CONCLUSIONS

- Group your subjects' responses into categories. *Examples:* personal items (clothing, jewelry); household items (furniture, plants); insects; action-oriented items (bat, boat, bike); passive items (statue, spoon). Then compare male and female responses to find out if either gender favors certain categories.
- How might people's experiences with everyday objects account for the different ways they perceive the pictures?
- What else might explain the differences in perception?

EXPLORE MORE

- Repeat the experiment, comparing other groups. *Examples:* adults to children, teachers to students.
- Repeat the experiment, only this time make it a multiple choice test. You might use some of the descriptions from the Possibilities list on page 90. *Example:* "Is #1 a butterfly or a bow?" Record and categorize responses. Compare results to the original experiment.

WHY IT MATTERS TO YOU

- This experiment reminds you that there can be two right answers to the same question—or two right perceptions of the same thing.
- People assign their own meanings to the things that surround them. One person might be terrified of mice while another person thinks they are cute. What would life be like if everyone saw everything in exactly the same way?

DID YOU KNOW?

- When similar experiments were done using a picture that could be a centipede, brush, comb, or teeth, most males saw it as a centipede or a brush, while most females saw it as a comb or teeth. Shown a picture of a small circle within a larger one, most males saw a target and most females saw a dinner plate. An equal number of males and females saw a ring or a tire. Shown a picture that could be a head or a cup, most males saw a head and most females saw a cup. See if you get similar results when you turn this into an experiment.

- When males and females were asked to choose words from a word list to describe the feeling of "grief," males chose "high," "red," "strong," "rough," and "angular," while females chose "low," "green," "weak," "smooth," and "rounded." (On this test, their descriptions were very similar for most other words.)
- Because perceptions are influenced by our everyday experiences, some tests have been found to be unfair to certain groups of people. *Example:* Since boys are encouraged to work on bicycles and cars, a test item showing a picture of gears and asking which way they turn may unfairly favor boys. Can you think of examples like this on tests you have taken?
- When males and females are asked to identify which of the letters and numbers at the right are "masculine" ("M") and which are "feminine" ("F"), they give very similar answers. Why do you think this happens? (You can turn this into another experiment.)

4	**A**	**S**	**T**
M F	M F	M F	M F
8	**9**	**6**	**K**
M F	M F	M F	M F
	7	**Q**	
	M F	M F	

ANSWERS: Most people say that S, 8, 9, 6, and Q are feminine and 4, A, T, K, and 7 are masculine.

WHAT IS IT?

1. 

2. 

3. 

4. 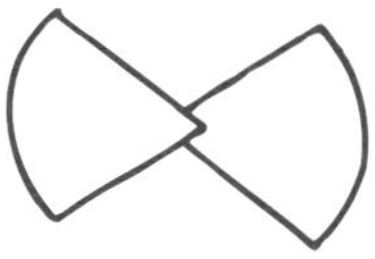

5. 

6. 

7. 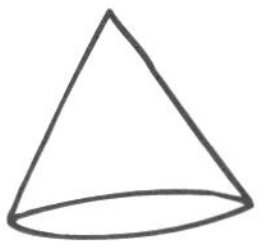

8. 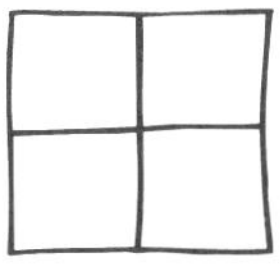

9. 

10. 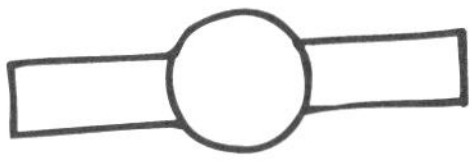

PEOPLE IN GROUPS

Does Competition Improve Performance?

Does competition make you work harder and faster to beat the other person? Or does it just cause hard feelings between people? This experiment compares competing with noncompeting performances of a simple sorting task.

SUBJECTS

- You and a friend

WHAT YOU NEED

- 1 package of regular toothpicks and 1 package of colored toothpicks, divided in half and mixed together in 2 piles
- 2 timers or watches with second hands
- Paper and pencils for your subjects
- A third person to time you (optional)
- Paper and pencil for recording observations and results, or a copy of the Experiment Data Sheet on page 7

WHAT TO DO

Part I: Noncompeting

1. Take 1 mixed-up pile of toothpicks and give your friend the other pile. Go into separate rooms. Sort the toothpicks, making separate piles for the regular (natural-colored) ones and each of the colors. Do this as quickly as you can. Notice how long it takes you and record your time.
2. Mix up the toothpicks and repeat.

Part II: Competing

1. Sort the toothpicks in the same room at the same time as your friend. See who can finish first. (You may want to have a third person time you.) Record your time.
2. Mix up the toothpicks and repeat.

CONCLUSIONS

- Compare your noncompeting times to your competing times. Did competition improve your performance?

EXPLORE MORE

- Repeat this experiment with several pairs of people. Have some of them do the competing part first and the noncompeting part second. This way you can tell if improvement in sorting speed is a result of practice.

WHY IT MATTERS TO YOU

- Although competition can be a powerful motivator, sometimes your best performances come when you are doing something for its own sake.
- Most people have a strong need for approval. They also have a strong desire to win. This can cause internal conflict, especially for people who are talented in many areas. They may sometimes do less than their best because they feel that always winning might lead to loss of approval. Have you ever experienced this internal conflict? Have you ever done less than your best? What happened as a result? Was it worth it?

DID YOU KNOW?

- Competition in the classroom can cause all kinds of problems. Students may lose sight of the true goal of learning. They may do anything to win, even cheat. They may decide that winning is impossible and give up on school. One way to avoid competition problems is to reward students for improving so they compete against themselves.
- Competition motivates people to perform faster, but often the quality of their performance suffers. Would you rather eat food that was inspected quickly or thoroughly? Would you rather ride in an airplane built quickly or built slowly and carefully?
- A runner does better against another runner than against the clock. So does a race horse; so does a rat running a maze.
- According to Deborah Tannen, author of the best-selling book *You Just Don't Understand: Women and Men in Conversation* (Morrow, 1990), males are more likely to see conversation as a form of competition—a way to get what they want. To females, conversation is a way to create closeness between and among people. Do you agree with Deborah Tannen's conclusions?
- Gifted children often learn better alone than in a group.

Are Some People More Cooperative than Others?

You may not get what you want all the time, but if you are lucky, you will get what you need—or so the saying goes. This experiment deals with a problem/puzzle that can't be solved unless the subjects decide to cooperate with one another. See how this decision to cooperate comes about and how long it takes your subjects to learn to work together.

SUBJECTS

- 5 people of similar ages and abilities

WHAT YOU NEED

- 6 pieces of stiff paper or thin cardboard for making a puzzle set
- Scissors
- Colored markers (red, green, blue, orange, and purple)
- 5 manila envelopes, 7 1/2" x 10" (or any size that will hold the puzzle pieces)
- A timer or clock with second hand
- Paper and pencil for recording observations and results, or a copy of the Experiment Data Sheet on page 7

WHAT TO DO

1. Follow the instructions on page 99 to make your puzzle set.
2. Give each subject an envelope with the puzzle pieces inside. Say, "Your goal is to make 5 perfect squares using all of the puzzle pieces. There are several combinations of puzzle pieces that will make 1 or 2 squares, but there is only 1 combination that will make 5 squares. The puzzle has not been solved until each person has a perfect square and all squares are the same size."
3. Say, "There are 3 rules everyone must follow. RULE 1: You may not speak at any time while you are working on the puzzle. RULE 2: You may not signal in any way that you want a particular puzzle piece. RULE 3: You may give puzzle pieces to others, but you may not take puzzle pieces."
4. Make sure that everyone understands the goal and the rules, then begin. Time how long it takes your subjects to complete the puzzle.

How to Make Your Puzzle Set

1. Cut five 6" squares out of stiff paper or cardboard.
2. Cut the squares into pieces and code them RED, GREEN, BLUE, ORANGE, and PURPLE, as shown.
3. Label each envelope with one of the colors (red, green, blue, orange, purple). Put the puzzle parts coded RED in the envelope labeled RED, the puzzle parts coded GREEN in the envelope labeled GREEN, and so on. You will have 5 sets of puzzle pieces.

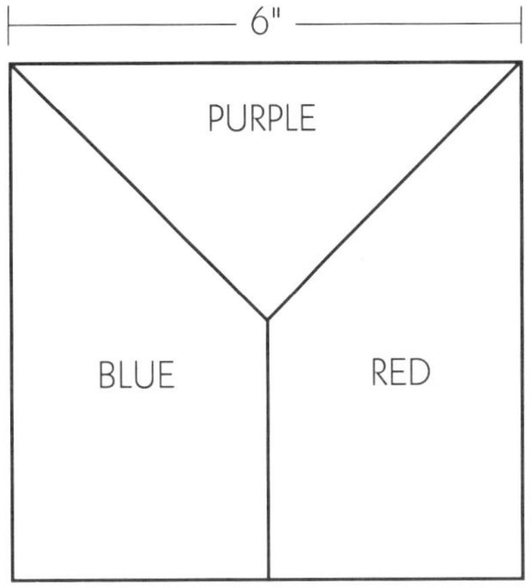

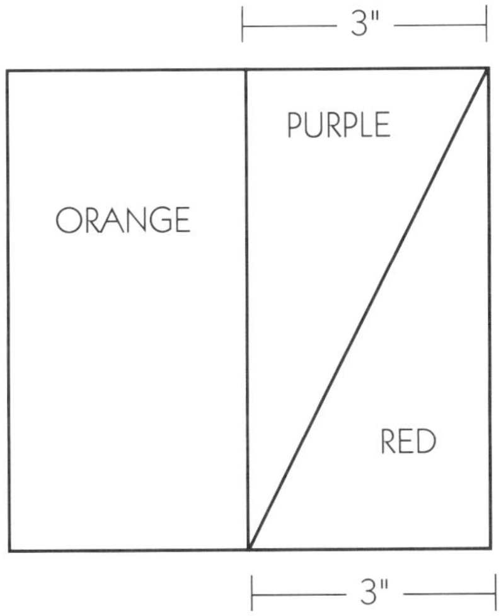

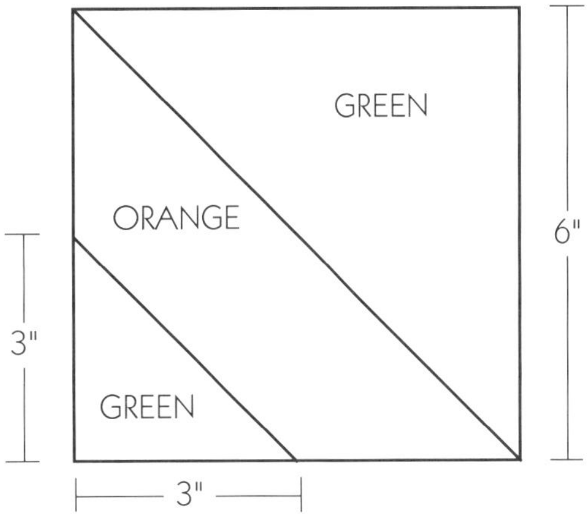

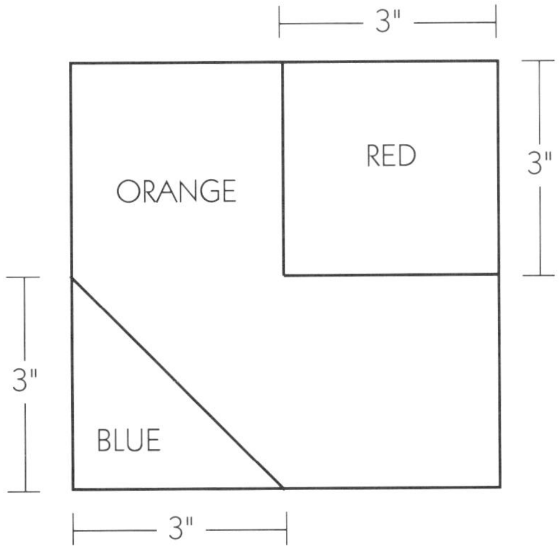

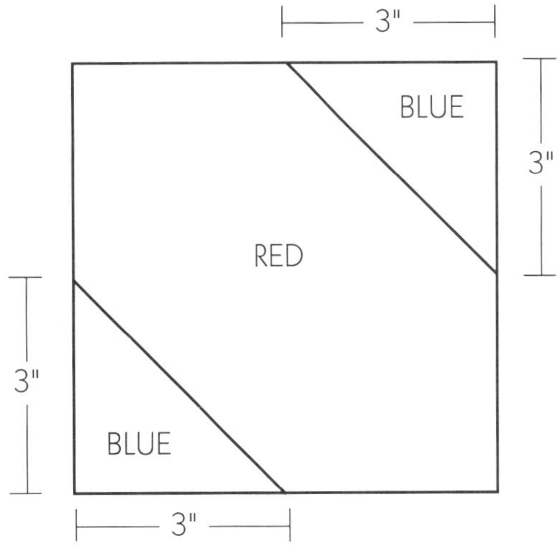

CONCLUSIONS

- What did you notice about the way the people solved the puzzle? Were some subjects more cooperative than others? Did some try to take the pieces they needed?

EXPLORE MORE

- Repeat this experiment with different groups of people. *Examples:* all males, all females, all adults, all children, etc. Compare results. What conclusions can you draw?

WHY IT MATTERS TO YOU

- When we have a problem to solve, it seems natural to take what we need from others. We look for people who can help us. But how often do we volunteer to help someone else solve a problem? You may have the missing piece to someone else's "puzzle," if you take time to notice. Maybe someone else will notice that he or she has a piece you need.

DID YOU KNOW?

- Going after what you want may seem like the key to meeting your needs. But consider this: The most successful businesses are those that figure out what *other people* want and need. In other words, if you really want to succeed in life, you have to think about other people, too.
- Communication is based partly on what we think is going on. We understand only about 70% of the words we hear and fill in the rest. *Example:* Someone asks you, "Did you shake with fear?" But you're hungry and thinking about dinner, so what you hear is, "Did your steak taste rare?" It's easy to misunderstand what someone else is saying when we're thinking about other things.

Castlegate: A Cooperative Brain Teaser

Once upon a time there were twin princes who were always trying to outdo each another. Their father, the King, tried everything to get them to cooperate. He offered rewards and threatened punishment, but nothing was closer to the princes' hearts than winning.

The King could not change them while he was alive, but while he was dying, he came up with a plan. In his last wishes, he ordered his sons to ride their horses to the edge of the Kingdom and back to the castle again, dismounting only once to water their horses. The son whose horse arrived at the castle gate *second* would inherit the entire Kingdom.

The sons began their race. Each tried to ride more slowly than the other. After two days and two nights of riding ever more slowly, the princes grew weary. It seemed as if neither would ever arrive back at the castle gate.

Exhausted, they stopped for the night at a roadside inn. The innkeeper awakened them the next morning so they could leave together. As they were getting ready to leave, one brother whispered something into the other brother's ear. They both laughed, jumped into the saddles, and rode as fast as they could to the castle gate.

What words did the one brother whisper in the other brother's ear?

Answer: "Let's trade horses!"

Do Children and Adults Group People Differently?

The older we get, the more ways we have to define, describe, and categorize people. The more people we know, and the more we know about people, the more we see them in different ways. Think back to when you were very young. Did most people seem very similar to you? This experiment explores how children and adults tend to group people.

SUBJECTS

- At least 3 young children who understand the concepts of "alike" and "different"
- At least 3 adults

WHAT YOU NEED

- Magazines with pictures of all types of people—men, women, boys, girls, tall people, short people, heavy people, thin people, people of different races, etc.
- Scissors
- Index cards
- Glue
- Paper and pencil for recording observations and results, or a copy of the Experiment Data Sheet on page 7

WHAT TO DO

Do this experiment with one group (children or adults) at a time. It doesn't matter who goes first.

1. Cut out several people pictures. Glue them onto index cards so they won't get too crumpled during the experiment.
2. Ask your subjects to group the pictures together, putting the ones that "go together" in different stacks. Don't answer any questions they might have about how to sort the pictures. Record the results.

CONCLUSIONS

- What categories do most people use to group the pictures? Age, race, gender, size, or...?
- Do children and adults group people differently?

EXPLORE MORE

- Give your subjects a list of occupations: Homemaker, Police Officer, Judge, Nurse, Singer, Basketball Player, Firefighter, Doctor, Psychologist, Secretary. Have them match the people pictures to the occupations. What conclusions can you draw from the results?

WHY IT MATTERS TO YOU

- This experiment reminds you to not put people in categories too quickly. It also reminds you to not let yourself get boxed in. If you are a girl who dreams of becoming a race car driver, and if you think that all race car drivers are men, don't let this stop you from pursuing your dream. (You wouldn't be the first female race car driver. Shirley "Cha-Cha" Muldowney was the first woman to race competitively in Top-Fuel 1/4-mile dragsters; Janet Guthrie was the first to qualify to race in the Indianapolis 500.) If you are a boy who wants to be a homemaker, don't rule it out because you think that all homemakers are women. (John Lennon, a former member of the rock group The Beatles, was a homemaker.) What matters is to do what *you* want and can do well.

DID YOU KNOW?

- Researchers have found that football and hockey teams that wear black uniforms are considered to be more aggressive and receive more penalties. Referees are more likely to charge aggressive plays as "malicious" when the players are dressed in black. Why do you think this happens?

How Do Individuals Come Together as a Group?

Can 4–5 people act as "one," even without a single person being appointed as leader? This experiment explores how people gradually start acting as a group—a single unit—rather than as separate individuals.

SUBJECTS

- 4–5 people

WHAT YOU NEED

- A timer or clock with second hand
- Paper and pencil for recording observations and results, or a copy of the Experiment Data Sheet on page 7

WHAT TO DO

1. Tell your subjects to stand and simply fold and unfold their arms until you tell them to stop. Have them do this for several minutes (at least 2). There will be no sense of "togetherness." It is likely to seem as if a long time is passing, and people will probably feel uncomfortable.
2. Tell your subjects to rest and relax for about 30 seconds.
3. Now tell them to fold their arms again and wait with their arms folded until they all unfold them at exactly the same time. They must do this without speaking. Don't give up if this doesn't work the first time. Have your subjects keep trying until they succeed.

CONCLUSIONS

- What usually happens during this experiment is that a lot of tension builds up, then everyone drops their arms at the same time. Some groups have to practice working together for a while before this becomes possible. When people work together for a period of time—for example, practicing team sports or rehearsing for a play—they gradually develop a sense of togetherness and are able to "read" one another. Part of this togetherness happens because they share a single goal.
- Ask your subjects how they felt when they were doing the experiment.
- Did body language play a part in the group coming together?
- Does one person seem to emerge as the group's leader?

EXPLORE MORE

- Repeat the experiment with a different group, but have your subjects close their eyes. Does this make it easier or more difficult for them to act as a group?
- Repeat the experiment with subjects standing closer together and farther apart. Which seems to work better?

WHY IT MATTERS TO YOU

- You may have experienced something similar to this experiment in busy traffic, when people and cars are able to move along fairly smoothly without bumping into one another. Are there other times and situations when this special form of communication might be valuable, even life-saving?
- A leader sets the pace and notices small changes before other people do. A leader sees the big picture and the ways in which many details are beginning to fit together to form a new trend or a new idea. He or she may not only be tuned into the direction the culture is moving, but may actually feel these changes inside as well. If you learn to pay attention to outside details and act on your strong inside feelings, you may increase your leadership abilities.

DID YOU KNOW?

- A university student made a short film (3 1/2 minutes) of children playing together on a school playground. One little girl seemed to be able to lead without even being aware of it. Whenever she jumped rope near a group of children, the other children began to match her rhythm in whatever they were doing—jumping rope, bouncing a ball, or just moving around. As the little girl went from group to group, she was leading the activity on the entire playground. The filmmaker matched the children's movements to a piece of contemporary music. Not a single frame was off the beat. The children all seemed to be moving together as if listening to inner music. Does this help to explain how a particular kind of music can "suddenly" become popular? Does it help to explain other group behaviors?

SELF-EXPRESSION

Do People Reveal Them-selves More in Their Art or in Their Writing?

There are many different ways we can learn what other people are like. Their clothes, their hairstyles, their ways of walking, their choices of foods or friends are just a few clues we may use. Are there some things that are especially revealing or tell us an unusual amount about another person? This experiment explores the question, "Which tells us more about a person, his or her artistic style or writing style?"

SUBJECTS

- At least 8 people who do not know one another well

WHAT YOU NEED

- 2 pieces of paper for each subject
- Pencils for your subjects
- Paper and pencil for recording observations and results, or a copy of the Experiment Data Sheet on page 7

WHAT TO DO

1. Ask your subjects to draw a picture on one piece of paper. Ask them to write a short paragraph on the other piece of paper.
2. Collect the papers and mix them up.
3. Give a drawing and a paragraph to each subject. (Make sure that subjects don't get their own drawings or paragraphs.) Ask them to look at the drawings and paragraphs and see if they can tell anything about the artists/authors.

   The drawing and paragraph may or may not belong to a single artist/author. Ask your subjects to "analyze" each artist/author based on the work and to write their insights on the papers. You might ask them to comment on whether the artist/author is male or female, old or young, happy or sad most of the time, more serious or more playful, etc.
4. Have your subjects find and take back their own drawings and paragraphs. Ask them to rate how accurate the "analyses" are, using a scale of 0 ("it doesn't fit me at all") to 5 ("it sounds a lot like me").

CONCLUSIONS

- Did each artist/author get similar readings of his or her personality for the drawing and the paragraph, or were the two readings very different? If they were different, how might this be explained?
- Which seems to reveal more about a person—drawing, writing, or neither?
- Would you expect some people to express themselves better through drawing? Would you expect some to express themselves better through writing? Why? Can you think of other ways in which people might express themselves even better?

EXPLORE MORE

- Repeat this experiment, comparing students who are very good at art with students who are very good at math.
- Turn the experiment around. Take the analyses your subjects wrote about one another, mix them up, hand them out, and have your subjects draw a picture or write a paragraph that could have been created by the person described on the paper. For each paragraph they receive, they should draw a picture. For each drawing they receive, they should write a paragraph.

WHY IT MATTERS TO YOU

- When you look at a work of art or read a book, think about the person who created it. If you look closely or read carefully, you'll find that you can become well-acquainted with an artist or author you've never met.
- Almost everything you do is a kind of self-portrait. Look at your room, your wardrobe, your hairstyle. They all express something about you. Do they say what you want them to say?

DID YOU KNOW?

- It's said that Leonardo da Vinci's famous painting, the *Mona Lisa,* may actually be a self-portrait. Look at some of da Vinci's art and some of another artist's art. What can you learn about each person from his or her work?

What Does Handwriting Reveal?

It's usually very easy to tell when someone has written something in a hurry. This experiment looks at what else, if anything, may be revealed by a person's handwriting.

SUBJECTS

- Any number of people

WHAT YOU NEED

- Copies of the What Does Handwriting Reveal? test on page 110, one for each subject
- Pencils for your subjects
- Paper and pencil for recording observations and results, or a copy of the Experiment Data Sheet on page 7

WHAT TO DO

1. Have your subjects take the What Does Handwriting Reveal? test. Ask them to sign their tests.
2. Collect the tests.

Answers to What Does Handwriting Reveal? Test

1. A (even lines may show an even mood, while lines that go up, then down, then up again represent someone who may be switching back and forth from happy to sad to happy, etc.)
2. B (can you tell why?)
3. B (the space between "am" and "20" shows hesitation)
4. A (the name of someone we respect may be written larger)
5. B (the letters get smaller in B, showing that the writer is not having to think as hard to come up with ideas)
6. A (girls around age 13 will often decorate their writing in this way)
7. B (B breaks the rules, while A stays in line; see "Did You Know?" on page 109)

CONCLUSIONS

- Did most of your subjects give the same answers? If so, this shows that we attach meaning to handwriting styles. Even if a person's handwriting doesn't tell much about him or her, we read meaning into it.

EXPLORE MORE

- Make a handwriting sample when you are sleepy or ill. Then make a sample of your regular handwriting and compare the two. Show the two samples to another person and ask if he or she can tell which sample you made when you were sleepy or ill.
- Draw a line quickly, then another line slowly. Show the two lines to other people and see if they can tell which is which.
- Think of something you feel angry about and write a sentence about it. Now think of something you feel happy about and write a sentence about it. Compare the two handwriting samples.

WHY IT MATTERS TO YOU

- Since other people form opinions and impressions of you from your handwriting, you may want to try improving it! Does your handwriting look organized, neat, and intelligent?
- Imagine that you are writing a paper for school. You could make it look neat, or you could make it look sloppy. Which choice would probably earn the higher grade?

DID YOU KNOW?

- A meaningful number—or a "statistically significant number"—of convicted felons do not line up their left margins when they are asked to write on a blank sheet of paper.
- In its official list of job descriptions, the U.S. Labor Department has moved the job of handwriting analysis from the "Amusement and Entertainment" category to the "Miscellaneous Professionals" category.
- People who have lost the use of their hands and must learn to write by holding a pen in their mouth have the same "handwriting" as when they were able to use their hands.

WHAT DOES HANDWRITING REVEAL?

Circle A or B for each question.

1. Who is changing back and forth from happy to sad?

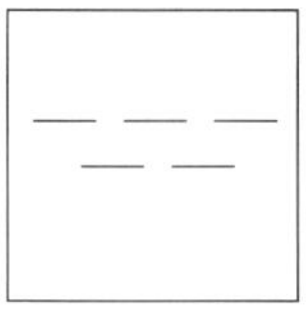
a

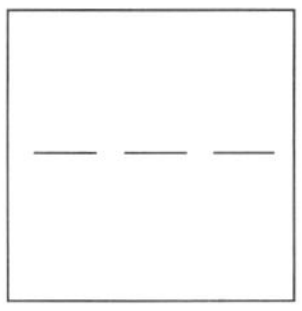
b

2. Who likes to be the center of attention?

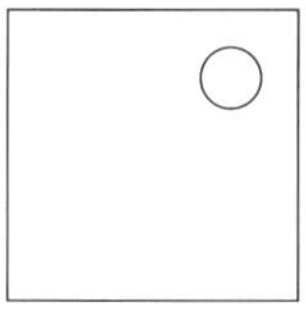
a

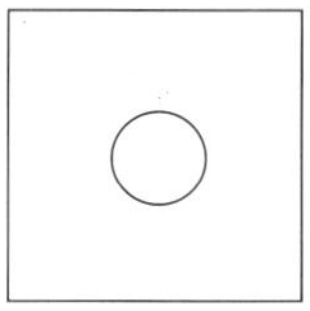
b

3. Who is unsure about how old he or she is?

a *I am 20 years old.*

b *I am 20 years old.*

4. Who really thinks that Mary will do a good job?

a *Mary Smith will do a good job.*

b *mary Smith will do a good job.*

5. Who is more intelligent?

a *I am smarter than you are.*

b *I am smarter than you are.*

6. Who is a 13-year-old girl?

a *My birthday is coming soon!*

b *My birthday is coming soon.*

7. Who is more likely to be writing from jail?

a

Dear Mom -
Thank you for the note - I was very glad to hear that all is well at home.
Please send me a care package that will include Cookies, soap and a photo of all of you.
Love -
Your #1 Kid!

b

Dear Mom -
Thank you for the note - I was very glad to hear that all is well at home.
Please send me a care package that will include Cookies, soap and a photo of all of you.
Love - Your #1 Kid!

Signature

Are We More Alike or More Different?

This is the second of two guest experiments in *Psychology for Kids II.* It was contributed by Stacy Dunn, who recently graduated from college and plans to get her master's degree. You'll learn more about Stacy in "Did You Know?" at the end of this experiment.

SUBJECTS

- 10 friends

WHAT YOU NEED

- 10 apples as close in shape, size, and color as possible
- Paper and pencil for recording observations and results, or a copy of the Experiment Data Sheet on page 7

WHAT TO DO

1. Invite 10 friends to get together.
2. Give each friend an apple. Tell them not to eat their apples.
3. Ask your friends to find the perfectly shaped apple among the 10 they have.

CONCLUSIONS

- Did everyone pick the same apple as having the perfect shape, or were there different opinions within the group?
- We all have our own ideas of the perfect apple. Similarly, we all have our own ideas about people.

EXPLORE MORE

- Make the experiment more involved by asking your subjects to identify the perfect size, color, smell, texture, and taste (this time they get to eat the apple!).
- Ask several people to tell you their idea of a perfect day. How many types of perfect days do you hear about?
- Photograph several people's bare feet. Label the pictures on the back. Show them to a group of subjects without revealing the labels. Ask questions like, "Can you tell who's tall? Who's blonde? Who's the oldest? Who's the youngest?" People will probably have a hard time answering these questions because we're more alike than we are different.

WHY IT MATTERS TO YOU

- What people may realize at the end of this experiment is that there are many more similarities than differences among apples...and also among people.

DID YOU KNOW?

- Stacy Dunn, who contributed this experiment, is a lot like you if you enjoy riding horses, going whitewater rafting, skiing, practicing martial arts, and participating in other challenging physical activities. But don't stereotype her or assume that Stacy is all play and no work. She does many other things, too—from her wheelchair. She is a motivational speaker, an advocate for people with disabilities, a Red Cross worker/trainer, a translator for a lawyer, and more. Stacy is a "good apple"!

Are People More Subjective or More Objective?

This experiment shows how sometimes people see the world from the "inside out" (from their own point of view) and sometimes they see the world from the "outside in" (from someone else's point of view).

SUBJECTS

- 4 or more people

WHAT YOU NEED

- Paper and pencils for your subjects
- Paper and pencil for recording observations and results, or a copy of the Experiment Data Sheet on page 7

WHAT TO DO

Do this experiment with 2 subjects at a time.

1. Give 2 of your subjects a math test. Read the following simple problems and have them write down the answers.
   - 7 – 4 =
   - 10 + 3 =
   - 12 x 3 =
   - 4 x 2 =
   - 9 x 3 =
2. Give your other 2 subjects a spelling test. Read the following words aloud and have them write down the correct spellings.
   - egg
   - free
   - teeny
   - bubble
   - eagle

3. After each test, tell your subjects to shut their eyes. Trace a *script* capital E on each person's forehead and ask them to write down what you traced. It's important that this be a script E because the edges are rounded—like a 3 in reverse. Do not say the letter while you are tracing it.

4. Ask each person to tell you what you traced on his or her forehead.

CONCLUSIONS

- Subjects who viewed the symbol from the "inside out" will report it as a 3. They saw the symbol *subjectively*—from their own point of view.
- Subjects who viewed the symbol from the "outside in" will report it as an E. They saw the symbol *objectively*—from someone else's point of view.
- Did the subjects who took the math test report the symbol as a 3 more or less often than those who took the spelling test?
- You might want to compare the results of this experiment with those of Experiment #10, "How Do People Make Judgments?," to see if you can draw any interesting conclusions.

EXPLORE MORE

- Repeat the letter-tracing part of the experiment without giving the tests.
- Use the experiment specifically to compare male and female responses.

WHY IT MATTERS TO YOU

- When you can look at things both from the "inside out" (subjectively) and from the "outside in" (objectively), you have the ability to appreciate other people's needs, problems, and perspectives. Do you take the time to look at things from other people's point of view? Do you look at things this way too often? Usually it's best to try to see things both ways.

DID YOU KNOW?

- Studies have shown that males are more likely than females to see the script E from the "outside in" (objectively)—as an E, not a 3.

BEHAVIOR

Can We Shape Other People's Behavior?

If you know something about how behavior is learned, you can use this knowledge to train your pets, "train your humans" (that is, get other people to treat you the way you want to be treated), and understand why people do some of the things they do. One way to train other people is by giving them rewards for behaving in ways you want them to behave. This experiment explores the use of rewards.

SUBJECTS

- 2 or more people

WHAT YOU NEED

- A few friends to act as observers
- Paper and pencil for recording observations and results, or a copy of the Experiment Data Sheet on page 7

WHAT TO DO

1. Assign one subject to play the part of the Hungry Lab Rat and the other to play the part of the Food Pellet Dispenser. The person playing the Rat leaves the room while you and the other observers decide on a behavior to be shaped or conditioned. You might choose something like having the Rat stand by the heater, sit in a particular chair, or look out a window.
2. Invite the Rat back into the room. Don't explain what you hope the Rat will do. Simply observe. When the Rat gets "warmer"—closer to performing the behavior you decided on—the Food Pellet Dispenser says "Good." This single word should be said in the same way every time, and nothing else should be said.
3. The experiment ends when the Rat performs the behavior you decided on.

CONCLUSIONS

- Did it seem as if the Rat was easy to train?
- Can you think of ways that shaping behavior might be used to improve relationships between people?
- Does this experiment give you any clues about how peer pressure might work to shape people's behavior?

EXPLORE MORE

- You have used verbal shaping if you have ever played the game of 20 Questions. Play it again, only this time look at it from a more scientific point of view. Here's how to play, if you don't already know: One person thinks of something and tells the other person the category—animal, vegetable, or mineral. The second person may ask 20 yes or no questions to find out what the other person is thinking of. Only questions that are answered "No" are counted, so the asker really has more than 20 questions.

WHY IT MATTERS TO YOU

- If you want to make friends with a certain person, try shaping his or her behavior. Smile at the person, speak to him or her in a friendly way, and so on whenever he or she comes in your direction or speaks to you in ways you want to hear. Use the person's name when you speak to him or her. Soon you may find this person coming around you more often.
- Think of someone you know who always seems to be in a bad mood. Maybe he or she simply isn't a nice person. But consider how you might be shaping his or her behavior. Do your own actions and reactions play a role in how others treat you or respond to you?
- Pay attention to how other people try to shape your behavior. Try to stay in charge of your own behavior. This means being aware of what you think and how you feel. It means being careful not to do things just to get approval or to avoid disapproval.

DID YOU KNOW?

- We shape other people's behavior whether we want to or not, whether we mean to or not. We train them when we respond to them in positive or negative ways. Sometimes we train other people in ways we don't mean to. *Example:* Some students didn't like the rules that their teacher made, so they decided to break them. They hoped that the teacher would eventually give up and stop expecting them to follow the rules. Instead, the teacher made even more rules. This certainly wasn't what the students wanted. But it's what they got because they "trained" their teacher to believe that they needed more rules.
- Some college students did an experiment to show how students can shape a teacher's behavior. When their professor went to one side of the room, the students looked interested in what he was saying. But when he went to another side of the room, the students looked bored. Before long, the professor was spending most of his time...can you guess where? The professor's behavior had been shaped by the students.

Helpful Hints about Rewards and Punishments

Are you trying to train a pet...or a family member or friend? Keep these hints in mind.

- Rewards or punishments must come immediately after the behavior you want to change.
- A swift and sure mild punishment is more effective than a delayed punishment, even if the delayed punishment is more severe. This is one reason why some young people smoke cigarettes or are careless about what they eat. They really don't believe that they will be the ones to get lung cancer or heart disease—and even if they do, it will happen when they are "old." The punishment is so far away that it has no effect on their behavior today.
- A reward is anything that makes a behavior occur more often—even if it seems like a punishment. This is why some people may repeat crimes. Going to prison is a reward to them because they have come to feel that prison is their home.
- Behaviors that are rewarded every time are learned very quickly. Behaviors that are rewarded only part of the time are learned more slowly, but are longer-lasting. If rewards are given every time, the subject tends to give up quickly when the rewards stop coming.
- If you are training your pet, offer praise along with a food reward. Eventually your pet will do the trick for the praise alone, and you won't have to give the food reward.
- Ignoring a behavior gets rid of it more permanently than punishment, but it takes longer. (See Experiment #35, "Will Ignoring a Behavior Make It Go Away?")
- Whether you use rewards or punishments, don't try to change more than one behavior at a time.

Can We Condition People to Respond in Certain Ways?

This experiment is similar to the game "Simon Says," in which people are supposed to follow instructions only if they start with the words "Simon Says." People who are playing this game often become conditioned to follow instructions even when the "Simon Says" order is not given. Of course, this is how they lose the game!

SUBJECTS

- As many people as you want to test

WHAT YOU NEED

- Paper and pencils for your subjects
- A ruler
- Paper and pencil for recording observations and results, or a copy of the Experiment Data Sheet on page 7

WHAT TO DO

Do this experiment with one subject at a time.

1. Ask your subject to sit at a desk with a pencil and a piece of paper. Explain that each time you say "Write," he or she should draw a line.
2. Stand behind your subject. Every time you say "Write," tap your subject's chair with the ruler. Do this 20 times.
3. For the 21st time, tap the ruler on the chair but don't say "Write."

CONCLUSIONS

- What happened when you tapped the ruler but didn't say "Write"? Did your subject start to draw a line or not?
- What do you think is going on in this experiment? What conclusions can you draw?

EXPLORE MORE

- If you hold a sheet of clear plastic in front of your face and have someone throw a crumpled piece of paper at you from the other side, it will make you blink. Design an experiment to make someone blink when they wouldn't normally do this.

WHY IT MATTERS TO YOU

- Understanding conditioned learning helps you to control habits you would rather not have. Ask yourself, "Is there anything related to my habit that I am doing automatically, without thinking about it? How does it contribute to my habit?" *Example:* Sometimes people who are overweight think that they aren't really eating a lot. When they pay closer attention to their behaviors, they are often surprised to find out that they eat whenever they watch TV. The TV is like a little voice saying "Simon Says," and they respond to it automatically, as they have trained themselves to do. If you have a habit you want to break, start by paying attention to your automatic behaviors.

- Do you have an automatic reaction to certain types of people? Maybe you have been trained this way. *Example:* If every red-headed person you have ever known has treated you badly, you may have an automatic reaction to any new red-headed person you happen to meet. If you get a negative feeling about someone you don't really know, ask yourself if you may be judging the person based on your past experiences rather than on his or her individual qualities.

DID YOU KNOW?

- Scientists trained cells in rats by turning on a light and a sound at the same time the rats were given egg whites. After the training period, the rats' cells became active when the light and sound were turned on, even *without* giving the rats egg whites. Can you imagine how someone might learn to be allergic to something?

Classical Conditioning: Pavlov's Dogs

A Russian scientist named Ivan Pavlov became famous for discovering that involuntary responses could be trained. He rang a bell whenever he fed the dogs who were the subjects of his experiment. Dogs naturally salivate in response to food. Pavlov found that he could ring the bell and the dogs would salivate to the bell tone even when he didn't offer food. This is called *classical conditioning.* Here's how it works.

1. Food causes a dog to salivate naturally and involuntarily. Food is an *unconditioned stimulus.*

Food Alone

Dog Salivates

2. A bell tone will not cause a dog to salivate naturally. A tone is a *conditioned stimulus.*

Tone Alone

Dog Doesn't Salivate

3. Pavlov paired food with a bell tone until the dog learned to connect the two.

PLUS Tone

Food

Dog Salivates

4. Finally the bell tone caused the dog to salivate, even without food.

Tone Alone

Dog Salivates

The ***unconditioned*** response = salivating in response to food

The ***conditioned*** response = salivating in response to tone

What Can We Learn from Mealworms?

This experiment uses mealworms rather than humans so you can see another side of psychology experiments. Psychologists often try to understand human behavior and learning based on experiments with animals. Can you guess why animals are easier to use as subjects? Can you guess why the results of animal experiments aren't as useful?

Mealworms are fun to watch. Keep yours in a jar with a few handfuls of cereal or bran and a piece of apple or potato for water. Set them free at the end of the experiment.

SUBJECTS

- Mealworms (find them in piles of grain or sawdust, or purchase them from a bait shop or pet store for a small sum)

WHAT YOU NEED

- Food and water for your mealworms, and a place to keep them
- A sturdy cardboard gift box and lid, approximately 10" x 10" or 12" x 12" (the exact size doesn't matter as long as it isn't too small or too large)
- Posterboard or other stiff cardboard
- Glue or a glue gun
- Scissors
- A ruler
- A small amount of bran (in addition to the mealworms' regular food)
- Paper and pencil for recording observations and results, or a copy of the Experiment Data Sheet on page 7

WHAT TO DO

1. Follow the instructions on page 122 to build 2 T-mazes.
2. Put a teaspoon of bran at each of the 2 possible endpoints in both mazes.
3. Put two mealworms in each maze at the starting point.
4. Watch what they do.

How to Build Your Mealworm T-Mazes

1. Use the bottom of the cardboard gift box for one maze and the lid for the other maze.
2. Make the walls by cutting stiff cardboard strips about 3/4" wide. You will need 2 sets of walls.
3. Attach the walls to the floor of each maze. Use a glue gun instead of regular glue if you don't want to have to hold the walls while they are drying.

   Notice that in each maze you are forcing the mealworms to turn either right or left at the beginning, but giving them a choice at the end.

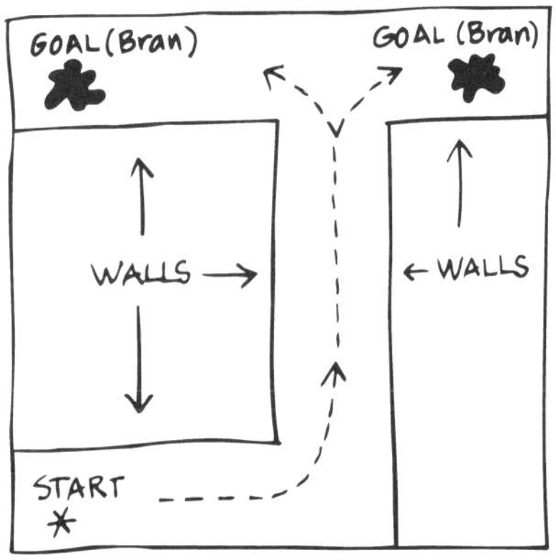

Forced Left Turn Maze

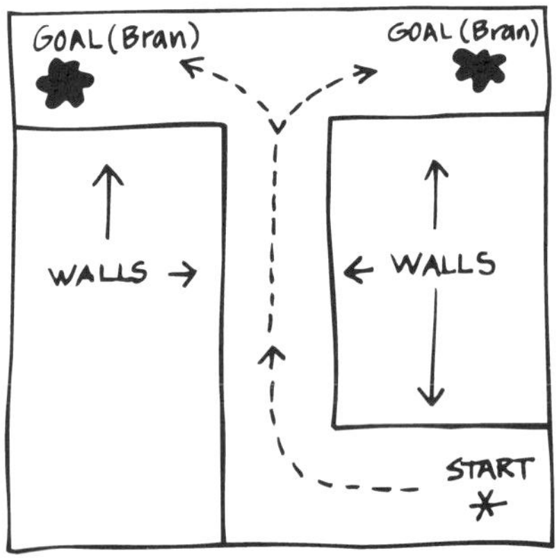

Forced Right Turn Maze

CONCLUSIONS

- Does forcing a mealworm to turn in a certain direction (right or left) make it more likely that the mealworm will turn in that same direction when given a choice (to reach the goal)?
- Did you get the results you expected?
- Compare this experiment with Experiment #10, "How Do People Make Judgments?" Can you draw any interesting conclusions?

EXPLORE MORE

- Build mazes of other shapes and test mealworms for other behaviors. *Example:* The Y-maze is simple to build and offers many possibilities for experimenting.

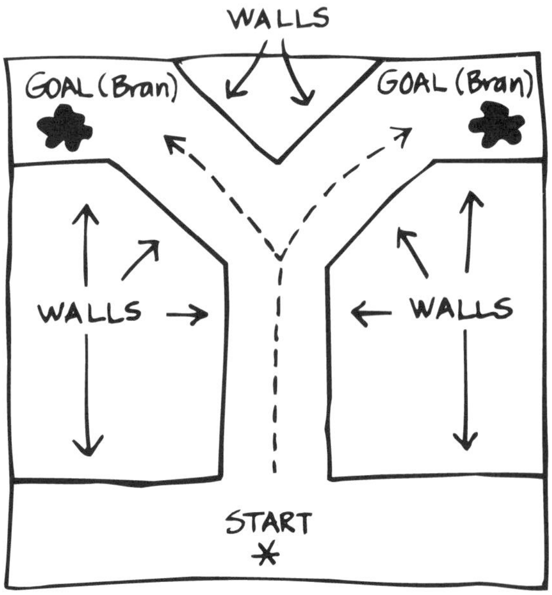

- Put mealworms in a simple shoebox and just watch what they do.
- Put 4 different colors of paper in a box, with a white circle in the center. Put mealworms on the white circle. See if you can find out what color(s) they prefer. Do you expect that they will prefer light colors or dark colors? Repeat this experiment using plain paper and patterned paper.

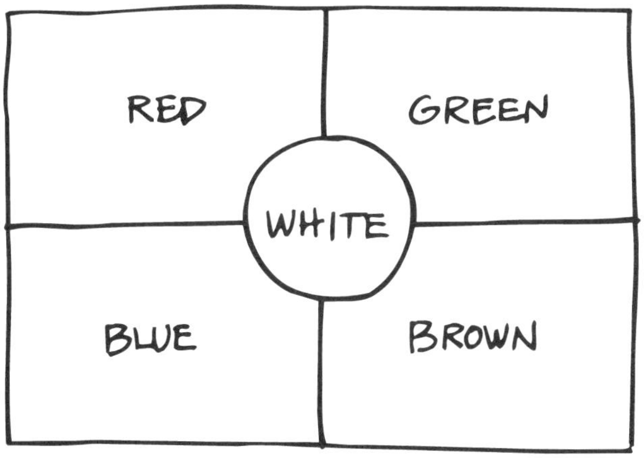

- Test the mealworms on different textures—slick paper, rough sandpaper, silk, etc. *Warning:* Don't use thick lamb's wool (like some car seat covers are made of). The worms will get tangled up in the fibers and die.

WHY IT MATTERS TO YOU

- When you do experiments like this one, you realize more fully that all creatures have preferences, behaviors, and habits. Those "ugly little worms" seem much more appealing after you do this experiment. It helps you to get over some of the "yecchhhh!" feelings you may have toward mealworms...and maybe other critters, too.

DID YOU KNOW?

- Speaking of getting over "yecchhhh!" feelings, psychologists can train people to overcome almost any fear by using a method called *desensitization*. It works like this: Let's say that you are afraid of rabbits. To desensitize you, a psychologist might begin by having you get comfortable with the closest thing to a real rabbit you could stand—perhaps a tin toy rabbit. Then you would move on to something closer to a real rabbit—perhaps a stuffed toy rabbit. Then you might move to seeing a real rabbit in a cage from a distance, and finally to actually petting a live rabbit.
- Many people share the fear of public speaking. How might you desensitize someone who has this fear?
- If there is something you fear or dread, see if you can think of ways to become more familiar with it and desensitize yourself. You might start by restating your feelings. Instead of saying "I hate (mice, horror films, the dark) or "I'm afraid of (mice, horror films, the dark)," you could try saying "I don't understand (mice, horror films, the dark)." When you admit that you don't understand something, you leave the door open to learn more about it and perhaps change your feelings.

Can We Use Rewards to Change Behavior?

Like Experiment #31, "Can We Shape Other People's Behavior?," this experiment explores the use of rewards, but in more detail. You learn about an important psychological concept called *operant conditioning.* Operant conditioning is when a subject is given a reward for performing a certain behavior. The reward makes it likely that the behavior will be repeated in the future...even without the reward being given.

If you didn't do Experiment #31, read "Helpful Hints about Rewards and Punishments" on page 118 before beginning this experiment. (Even if you did Experiment #31, you may want to reread the "Helpful Hints.")

SUBJECTS

- 1 pet or family member

WHAT YOU NEED

- A copy of the Learning Experiment I Sheet on page 127
- Paper and pencil for recording observations and results, or a copy of the Experiment Data Sheet on page 7

WHAT TO DO

1. Decide who your subject will be and what you want your subject to do. Choose a behavior that is possible and likely. For example, don't try to train your dog to speak French—it's not possible. Don't try to train your cat to play the piano—it's not likely.
2. Decide how to reward your subject. Choose a reward that will appeal to your subject. For example, don't reward your dog by buying her a new hat. Don't reward your brother by giving him a bone from the butcher.
3. Decide how you will determine when the new behavior is "there." How will you know when your training has succeeded?
4. Use the Learning Experiment I Sheet to define the terms of your experiment. Be very specific. See the example on the next page.

LEARNING EXPERIMENT I SHEET (Example)

1. SUBJECT (whose behavior will change?): My dog Spot.

2. THE BEHAVIOR IS NOW (be specific): Spot does not shake hands.

3. I WANT THE BEHAVIOR TO BE (be specific): When I point to Spot's right paw and say "Shake hands," Spot will lift his right paw at least two inches off the ground so I can shake it.

4. THE REINFORCEMENT WILL BE (what reward will you use? how will you give it?): One beef flavored dog treat, three pats on the head, and the words "Good dog!" all delivered each time and immediately after Spot lifts his paw. The first few times I will lift his paw, shake it, and give him the reinforcements.

5. THE BEHAVIOR HAS CHANGED WHEN (be specific): Spot shakes hands 2 times in a row without the dog treat when I point to his paw and say "Shake hands." I will still give him the pats on the head and say "Good dog!"

6. RESULT(S): Spot learned to shake hands through operant conditioning.

7. CONCLUSION(S): Behavior can be taught using positive reinforcement.

CONCLUSIONS

- It's easier to train your pet when you know the laws of behavior and how to use them.

EXPLORE MORE

- At one time, hardly anyone would have questioned the morality of training animals or of keeping animals as pets. However, some people are now questioning whether it's right for humans to train animals to do stunts—sometimes dangerous stunts—for our entertainment. Others are questioning whether people should even have animals as pets. It may be interesting for you to explore how people feel about this issue. Do they feel differently depending on the type of animal, or depending on what the animal is trained to do?

WHY IT MATTERS TO YOU

- The same laws that make it easy to train animals can also be used to "train" human beings. It's useful for you to know these laws of learning so you can observe your own behavior and recognize when you are being "trained" or manipulated by others.

DID YOU KNOW?

- It's not possible to train your pet to do everything you want, because some pet behaviors have to do with the animal's age or with certain natural needs the animal has. *Example:* A puppy has the natural need to chew at a certain stage of life and can't be housebroken until it reaches a certain age. When you know that your pet is following biology and not just being difficult, you will have more patience.

Operant Conditioning: Is This How Babies Learn to Smile?

It all starts one day when...

Then suddenly...

The adults respond with...
"Oh, look! How cute!
The baby smiled!
How adorable!"

Behavior ⟶ Reinforced ⟶ Is Learned

(smile) (praise) (repeated)

OPERANT CONDITIONING

LEARNING EXPERIMENT I SHEET

1. SUBJECT (whose behavior will change?):

2. THE BEHAVIOR IS NOW (be specific):

3. I WANT THE BEHAVIOR TO BE (be specific):

4. THE REINFORCEMENT WILL BE (what reward will you use? how will you give it?):

5. THE BEHAVIOR HAS CHANGED WHEN (be specific):

6. RESULT(S):

7. CONCLUSION(S):

Will Ignoring a Behavior Make It Go Away?

Does this sound familiar? Someone is bullying you, annoying you, or just making your life miserable. You want the behavior to stop. So you go to a parent, teacher, or other adult and complain. The adult says, "Just ignore [the person] and it will stop." And you think, *Sure it will*.... In fact, ignoring a behavior can be one way to make it go away. This experiment continues to explore the connection between rewards and behavior, but from a different angle.

SUBJECTS

- 1 pet or family member

WHAT YOU NEED

- A copy of the Learning Experiment II Sheet on page 132
- Paper and pencil for recording observations and results, or a copy of the Experiment Data Sheet on page 7

WHAT TO DO

1. Decide who your subject will be and what you want to train your subject to stop doing.
2. Decide how you have been reinforcing (rewarding) the behavior in the past. Decide how you will take away this reward.
3. Decide how you will determine when the old behavior is no longer "there."
4. Use the Learning Experiment II Sheet to define the terms of your experiment. Be very specific. See the example on the next page.

LEARNING EXPERIMENT II SHEET (Example)

1. SUBJECT (whose behavior will change?): My 13-year-old brother Bob.

2. THE BEHAVIOR IS NOW (be specific): Bob teases me by taking my books from my shelf and putting them on the floor. (*Note:* Bob may tease you in many ways, but you must select only *one* behavior to work on at a time.)

3. I WANT THE BEHAVIOR TO BE (be specific): That Bob stops taking my books; that they stay where I put them without Bob touching them.

4. THE REINFORCEMENT I WILL REMOVE IS (what reward will you stop using? how will you take it away?): I have been reinforcing Bob's behavior by yelling at him—giving him verbal attention. I will take away this reinforcement (my attention) by ignoring Bob when he takes my books from my shelf. I will quietly, calmly return the books to the shelf when Bob is not looking (or I will act like I would just as soon have them on the floor where he put them and leave them there).

5. THE BEHAVIOR HAS CHANGED WHEN (be specific): Bob does not take my books from my shelf for 5 days in a row.

6. RESULT(S): Bob has stopped teasing me by taking my books off the shelf.

7. CONCLUSION(S): Taking away the reinforcement/reward has helped to get rid of an unwanted behavior.

CONCLUSIONS

- Most of the time, your world responds to you in a fairly predictable way. There are paths that lead to the rewards you want. Being able to predict the likely results of your actions gives you some control over your life.
- You can use the knowledge of the laws of behavior to influence the world around you in powerfully positive ways. What if everyone around you and all of the governments of the world also understood the laws of behavior? What might be different? Probably just about everything!

EXPLORE MORE

- Choose a learning experience you are involved in. *Examples:* learning vocabulary words, math concepts, or gymnastics routines. Define the situation the way an experimenter might define it:
    - Describe your learning experience in clear, specific detail.
    - Tell what kind of learning is involved (verbal, physical, etc.)
    - Describe the reinforcers (rewards) that are present for you.
    - Tell how your performance changes from one "trial/time" to another.
    - Tell what kind of feedback you get.
    - Make a guess about changes in the learning procedure that would make your learning take place more quickly or more slowly. *Examples:* Remembering/not remembering to rest after practice; getting/not getting the proper feedback; having/not having the rewards follow immediately after the behaviors.
- How can this type of thinking help you to learn more efficiently?

WHY IT MATTERS TO YOU

- If certain people are bothering you, figure out how you are reinforcing/rewarding their behavior. Try to change your behavior. Often, people like this just want your attention. You might try giving them more attention when they are not bothering you.
- When a group of countries tries to change the policy or "behavior" of another country by agreeing that no one will trade goods with the "bad" country, this is similar to ignoring bad behavior in the hope that it will go away.
- Ignoring certain behaviors is a good way to make them stop. But it's important to remember that the behaviors will probably get worse before they get better or go away. At first, the annoying person (or pet) will try even harder to get a response from you. Now you know why this very useful way of changing a behavior isn't used as often as it might be. It takes patience! Also, some behaviors are impossible to ignore. Can you think of examples?

DID YOU KNOW?

- In one experiment, cooperative children were taught how to reward the wanted behaviors and ignore the unwanted behaviors of so-called "problem children." The cooperative children were then seated with the problem children in their sixth-grade classroom. Before long, the unwanted behaviors of the problem children disappeared because the other children were ignoring them.
- Rats who eat poisoned food will never again taste that particular kind of food, even when they don't get sick for hours after eating the food. This breaks 2 laws of learning: the law that says many trials are needed to condition a response, and the law that says reinforcement (negative or positive) must come immediately after a behavior.

- A child can learn a second language very easily up until about age 12 or 13. After that, it is nearly impossible to become fluent in another language. The laws of learning don't really explain this—nor do they completely explain human creativity, insight, and problem-solving.
- Compulsive gambling and other sensation-seeking behaviors have been found to be the result of low levels of the brain chemical called *norepinephrine.* Lack of norepinephrine leads to a low level of alertness and to boredom. To try to get rid of the boredom, a person seeks danger, which causes extra amounts of norepinephrine to be released into the brain.
- Depression is often related more to what is going on chemically *inside* your head than to anything that is going on *outside* of it.

What's In It for Them?

Why do some people do things that get them into trouble? What's in it for them? They don't seem to get any rewards—at least, not the obvious ones we usually think of. In fact, they may be getting "hidden rewards." See if you can figure out the hidden reward for each person's behavior in these examples.

1. Buddy the bully hits people on the playground, knowing that he will be sent to the principal's office, get into trouble at home, and be looked down upon by his classmates.
2. Sharon the shopkeeper comes to work late, although she knows she will get into trouble with her boss and may even lose her job, which she needs.
3. Tim and Tam the twins throw temper tantrums in the shopping mall, realizing that they will have to sit in the corner when they get home.
4. Ted eats a hot fudge sundae every day after school, even though he is very overweight and his social life is suffering.
5. Karla could easily get good grades, but she refuses to do even the minimum amount of studying. She may have to repeat a grade next year.

Some Possible Hidden Rewards

1. Buddy may feel more comfortable talking to the adults in the school office than playing games on the playground that seem silly and immature to him.
2. Sharon may secretly desire the courage to go out and look for a better job. She knows that if she gets fired, she will have no choice.
3. Tim and Tam may have found a way to make their parents take them home sooner when they are tired or bored. Or they may enjoy the attention they get when they throw temper tantrums.
4. Ted may have found a way to keep others at a distance and to avoid social interaction he finds difficult and uncomfortable.
5. Karla may have found a way to lower the expectations of her parents and teachers and to stay out of advanced classes, which require even more work.

Are there any negative behaviors you keep doing because of the hidden rewards?

LEARNING EXPERIMENT II SHEET

1. SUBJECT (whose behavior will change?):

2. THE BEHAVIOR IS NOW (be specific):

3. I WANT THE BEHAVIOR TO BE (be specific):

4. THE REINFORCEMENT I WILL REMOVE IS (what reward will you stop using? how will you take it away?):

5. THE BEHAVIOR HAS CHANGED WHEN (be specific):

6. RESULT(S):

7. CONCLUSION(S):

Can We Reward Creativity?

Rewards that come from the outside can influence behavior. But rewards also come from the inside. When something we do is rewarding all by itself, outside rewards can actually get in the way. This experiment explores what happens when we try to reward someone for being creative.

SUBJECTS

- Any number of people, divided into 2 groups of equal size (Group A and Group B)

WHAT YOU NEED

- Copies of the Creativity Test on page 135, one for each subject
- Pencils for your subjects
- Paper and pencil for recording observations and results, or a copy of the Experiment Data Sheet on page 7

WHAT TO DO

Test each group separately. Give each group 15 minutes to complete the Creativity Test.

1. Tell Group A that you are going to give them a Creativity Test. Explain that they should come up with as many creative answers as possible. Say that this test is for their enjoyment and will not be judged. Ask them not to write their names anywhere on their tests.
2. Tell Group B that you are going to give them a Creativity Test. Explain that they should come up with as many creative answers as possible. Say that their work will be judged, and the most creative responses may be rewarded. Ask them to write their names on the back of their tests.
3. Collect the tests and review each one. Give 2 points for every answer that seems especially creative to you. You might give points for answers that are unique—unlike anybody else's answers.

CONCLUSIONS

- After you score the tests, check to see which ones have names on the back. Are these the most creative tests or the least creative tests? Did the possibility of earning rewards seem to help, hinder, or have no influence on creativity?
- If rewards don't work to strengthen creativity, what might work?
- Is it possible that creative people are naturally less responsive to rewards than other people?

EXPLORE MORE

- Check into the lives and works of some great artists, composers, performers (including rock-and-roll stars), and writers. Do you find any hints that outside rewards hurt their creative work or brought them unhappiness?
- One study found that children who were rewarded for playing certain games became less interested in those games. (You can turn this into another experiment.)

WHY IT MATTERS TO YOU

- Think about times when you were rewarded for doing something you enjoyed. Did your creative play start to feel more like work?

DID YOU KNOW?

- In one study that involved elementary school children, professional artists, and writers, they all became less creative when they thought they were working for an outside reward.
- In another study, chimpanzees were busily painting with art supplies they were offered—until rewards entered the picture. Then the paintings became fewer in number and of poorer quality.
- We assume that all positive behaviors should be rewarded. In fact, there are times when rewards should not be used. Can you think of examples from your own life?

CREATIVITY TEST

1. Improve on these sneakers in as many ways as possible to boost sales.

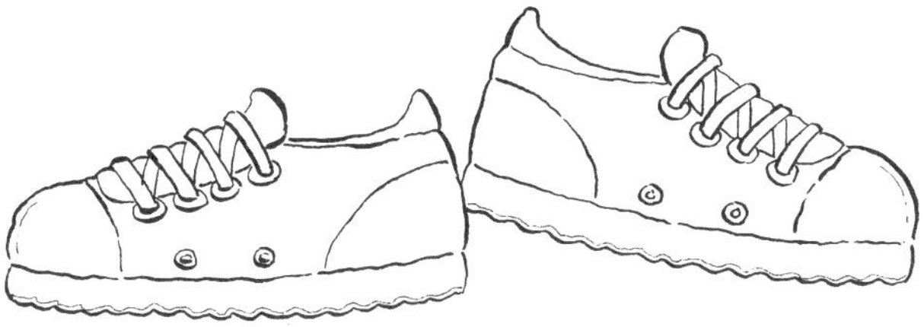

2. Give this picture a creative title.

____

3. Answer these three questions:

   A. How is time like spaghetti?

____

____

____

   B. How is a supermarket like an art museum?

____

____

____

   C. How is life like a board game?

____

____

____

4. Fill in the blanks: "Life is like ______________________________

because ______________________________."

Are Rewards and Success the Same?

Often rewards are mistaken for success. This is one reason why a rich and famous person can be unhappy. While the person may have received many rewards, he or she may not be experiencing a feeling of success.

SUBJECTS

- Enough people to divide into 3 groups to play 3 separate board games (your subjects should be about the same age and ability level for playing games)

WHAT YOU NEED

- 3 games: one that is too easy for your subjects, one that is just right for your subjects, and one that is much too hard for your subjects (*Example:* For 15-year-olds, you might choose Candyland [too easy], Monopoly [just right], and Bridge [too hard if they have never played it before])
- A timer or clock
- Copies of the Game Rating Form on page 138, one for each subject
- Pencils for your subjects
- Paper and pencil for recording observations and results, or a copy of the Experiment Data Sheet on page 7

WHAT TO DO

Put each group of game players in a separate room or separate parts of the same room. Don't let them see what the other groups are playing or they might guess the purpose of the experiment.

1. Give one group the too-easy game, one group the just-right game, and one group the too-hard game.
2. Tell each group that they can keep playing the game as long as they are enjoying themselves—up to 45 minutes. Explain that they must play for at least 20 minutes.

CONCLUSIONS

- Note the times when each group stops playing.
- When all of the groups are finished playing, give each player a Game Rating Form to fill out. Encourage them to add comments. Collect the forms and read the responses. What conclusions can you draw?

EXPLORE MORE

- Try doing some too-easy, just-right, and too-hard word puzzles or jigsaw puzzles. How did you feel about doing them? Did you feel proud and successful when you completed the too-easy puzzles? Did you feel good or bad about trying to solve a puzzle that was obviously impossible for you to do?

WHY IT MATTERS TO YOU

- If you are gifted and talented, you are familiar with the experience of receiving rewards, awards, and praise for things you didn't really have to work that hard to do. You are also familiar with the frustration of having to pretend to learn material you already know. This experiment can help you to explain these feelings to someone who hasn't experienced them personally.

DID YOU KNOW?

- Michael Jordan could have kept playing basketball. Instead, he found a new challenge: baseball. He seems to know the difference between rewards and success. How does this make him a good role model?
- Mental boredom may contribute to disease. Studies have found higher cancer rates among people who do not have enough challenges to meet their level of intelligence.
- An average learner requires 8 exposures to new materials in order to learn them. A gifted learner requires only 2 exposures to learn the same material. What is the gifted learner doing while the average learner is learning?
- Brain researcher Dr. Marian Diamond placed young rats in an enriched environment where they could explore and learn. The outer layers of the rats' brains actually got thicker.

Rewards vs. Success

Rewards...

1. come from the outside.
2. are given at the end of a performance, project, etc.
3. have to do with what the world likes to see you do.
4. may or may not come from doing something that challenges you.

Success...

1. is felt inside.
2. is experienced at any stage of a project or performance, not only at the end.
3. comes from your own goals and what you are trying to get done.
4. requires that you feel at least a little challenged by what you are doing. There should be at least a remote possibility that you might fail.

GAME RATING FORM

The name of the game you played:

____

RATINGS

How did you feel while you were playing the game? Give each of these feelings a rating from 0–5, depending on how strongly you experienced it while you were playing.

0 = I didn't feel it at all **5 = I felt it powerfully**

FEELING	RATING
1. Frustration	____
2. Success	____
3. Boredom	____
4. Pride	____

YES OR NO?

Did you win the game?	YES	NO
Do you care?	YES	NO

OTHER COMMENTS:

____

____

____

____

____

MEMORY AND LEARNING

Do We Learn More When We Rest Between Practices?

You've heard the saying, "Practice makes perfect." But there are many different ways to practice. Are some ways "more perfect" than others? This experiment compares two different ways of practicing. Which one is better?

SUBJECTS

- 2 people (subject A and subject B)

WHAT YOU NEED

- 5 pieces of paper for each subject, numbered #1, #2, #3, #4, and #5 (10 pieces in all)
- Pencils for your subjects
- A timer or clock with second hand
- Paper and pencil for recording observations and results, or a copy of the Experiment Data Sheet on page 7

WHAT TO DO

Test each subject separately.

1. Allow 60 seconds for each subject to write the alphabet backwards.
2. For subject A: Repeat 5 times, with 45-second rests in between. Give your subject a new piece of paper each time. (Start with #1, then #2, etc.)
3. For subject B: Repeat 5 times, with no rests in between. Give your subject a new piece of paper each time. (Start with #1, then #2, etc.)
4. Time each trial. Measure and graph the improvements. Which subject is able to write the alphabet backwards faster by the end of the experiment?

Sample Results Graphs

Your graphs might look something like this:

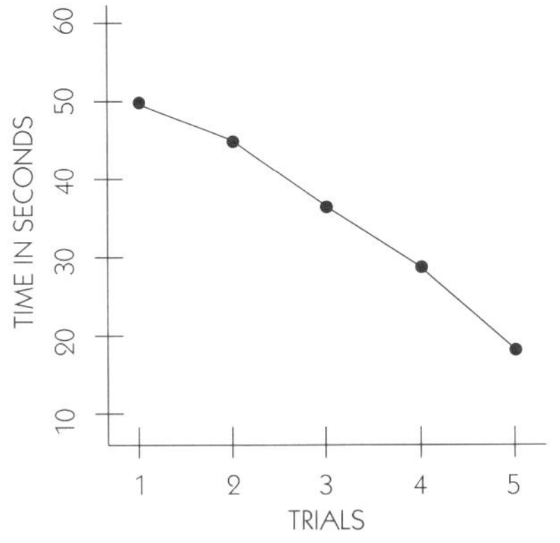

Subject A (rests between trials)

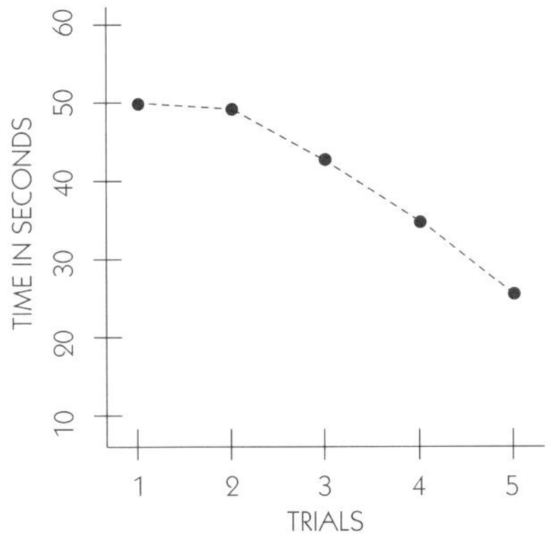

Subject B (no rests between trials)

Or you can plot your results on a single graph, like this:

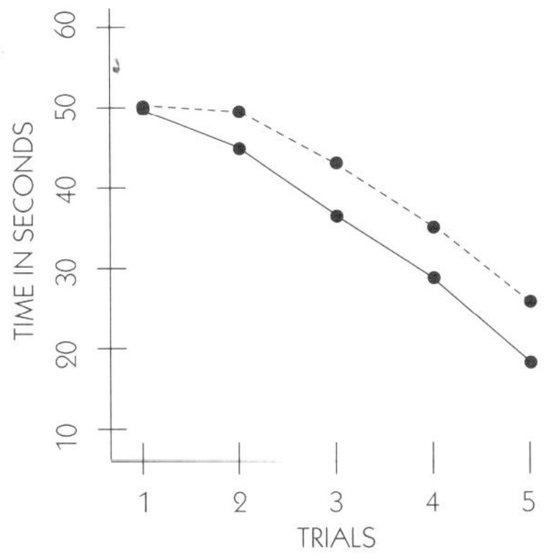

Subject A = solid line
Subject B = dotted line

CONCLUSIONS

- Usually the subject who rests between trials improves his or her time faster than the other subject. Why might this be true?

EXPLORE MORE

- Repeat this experiment with 2 more people, in case your results were caused by your first 2 subjects having different abilities. The more times you repeat the experiment, the more accurate or true your results will be.
- Repeat this experiment with a physical task, such as stringing popcorn or throwing crumpled paper into a wastebasket basketball-style.

WHY IT MATTERS TO YOU

- What you learn from this experiment can help you to practice sports, study, rehearse for a play, or practice a musical instrument more effectively, with better results. Constant practice is more work—and it doesn't work as well.

DID YOU KNOW?

- If you force yourself to keep practicing something even when you're tired and start making mistakes, you create even more work for yourself: You have to unlearn what you learned during the bad practice.

Is It Easier to Remember Something Meaningful?

A good memory makes life easier. This is probably why so many studies have been done to find out why people are able to remember some things better than other things. This experiment explores how meaning influences memory.

SUBJECTS

- 2 groups of people (Group A and Group B), with the same number in each group

WHAT YOU NEED

- Paper and pencils for your subjects
- Paper and pencil for recording observations and results, or a copy of the Experiment Data Sheet on page 7

WHAT TO DO

Test the two groups individually.

1. Tell Group A, "Please write 'Group A' at the top of your paper. I am going to read a list of words. When I am finished reading them, please write down as many as you can remember, in any order. Don't pick up your pencil until I have finished reading the list." When everyone is ready, read aloud the following list of words:

- cute
- smart
- small
- polite
- grim
- orange
- wrinkled
- tiny
- sweet
- honest
- sad
- strong
- odd
- interesting
- practical

2. Tell Group B, "Please write 'Group B' at the top of your paper. I am going to read a list of words. When I am finished reading them, please write down as many as you can remember, in any order. Don't pick up your pencil until I have finished reading the list." When everyone is ready, read aloud the following list of words:

- cute
- smart
- small
- polite
- grim
- peanut
- butter
- jelly
- sweet
- honest
- sad
- strong
- odd
- interesting
- practical

CONCLUSIONS

- It's usually easier to recall the first or last words on a list like this one, harder to recall words in the middle. But on the list you read to Group B, the normally forgettable middle has 3 words that go together: "peanut," "butter," and "jelly." Group B should recall these words more often than Group A recalls the 3 unrelated words ("orange," "wrinkled," and "tiny") in the middle of the list you read to them.

EXPLORE MORE

- Ask a friend to do an experiment with you. Say aloud any 3 letters of the alphabet you choose. Then immediately ask your friend to count backwards by 3's from 100 (100, 97, 94, 91...). Wait 20 seconds and ask your friend to repeat the 3 letters you said aloud. Your friend may have forgotten the letters because the task of counting interfered with his or her memory.
- Try this experiment again with another friend, only this time say aloud 3 words instead of letters. See if this makes a difference.

WHY IT MATTERS TO YOU

- You can improve your chances of remembering new information if it goes together in a meaningful way. Try to make unrelated things seem related when you learn them.
- The less activity or interference that goes on between learning and a test, the more you will remember at test time. This means that when you have an important test the next day, study right up until bedtime. After you finish studying, try to do as little as possible before you go to bed. If you have a test in one subject, don't study other subjects after you study for the test. Any additional studying will interfere with what you want to remember for the test.

DID YOU KNOW?

- It's easier to remember something if you are in the same room or situation you were in when you learned it originally. Try studying for a test while wearing the same clothes you'll wear when you take the test. See if this helps you to recall the information you need.

Are You Learning What You Think You're Learning?

Subjects of an experiment learned that they would earn rewards when they chose Card B instead of Card A.

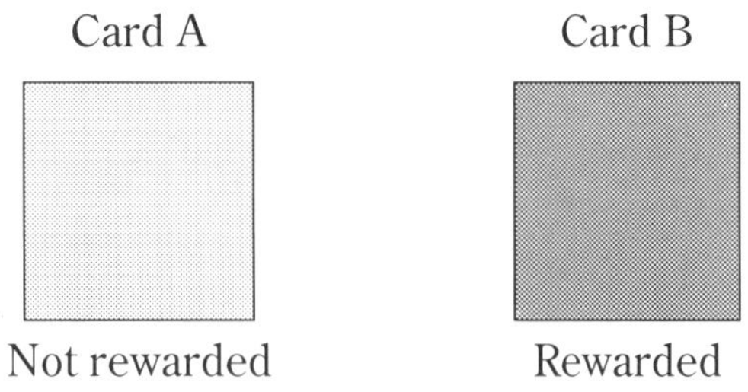

In the next part of the experiment, they were shown Card B and Card C.

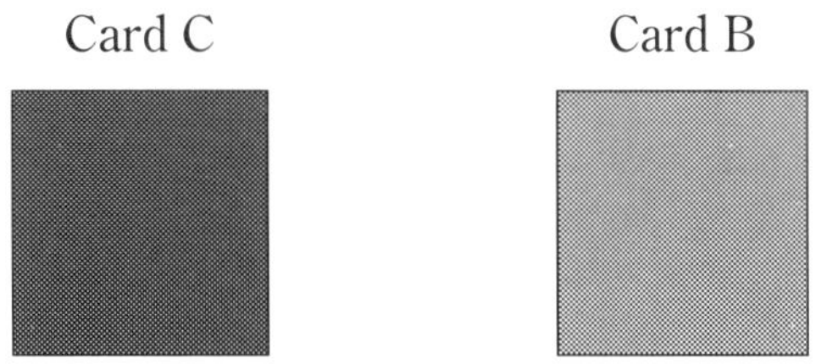

Which did they choose?

Did the subjects stick with Card B, the one they had "learned" to choose? No. They chose Card C, the darker of the two.

They had not really learned to choose Card B. Instead, they had learned to choose the darker of any pair of cards. (During the experiment, the cards were moved around so the same one was not always on the right or the left. Otherwise, we wouldn't know if the subjects might have learned to pick the card on the right or the card on the left.)

Similarly, when a child is spanked for doing something, we may think that the child is learning not to do that particular thing. In fact, the child may be learning that big people can make little people do what they want by using physical force.

Is Helplessness a Learned Behavior?

People who come to believe that what they do has little or no effect on their surroundings may simply give up on life and quit trying. Instead of being raised where rewards can be earned or punishments avoided, some people grow up where rewards and punishments come at odd times and seem unrelated to what they have or haven't done. They can't figure out the rules of the game because the rules change from one time to the next.

SUBJECTS

- 2 groups of people (Group A and Group B), with the same even number of people in both groups (you'll divide them into pairs)

WHAT YOU NEED

- Paper and pencils for your subjects
- A timer or clock
- Scissors
- A set of "helplessness cards" (see page 147) for each pair of players from Group B
- Paper and pencil for recording observations and results, or a copy of the Experiment Data Sheet on page 7

WHAT TO DO

1. Divide each group into pairs. Explain that they will play tic-tac-toe for 15 minutes.
2. Tell Group A that they will play under the normal rules: Whoever is first to complete a line of X's or O's (horizontally, vertically, or diagonally) wins that particular game.
3. Tell Group B that they will play under special rules. Say: "At the end of a game, you will turn over a card that will say who the winner is." Give each pair of players from Group B a set of "helplessness cards" turned face down. Explain that if they use all the cards, they should shuffle them and use them again.
4. Instruct the groups to start playing. Call "Time" when the 15 minutes are up.

CONCLUSIONS

- Discuss with both groups what happened while they were playing. Did anyone get bored? How did they play? How did they feel during the game? Did anyone lose interest in trying to line up their X's and O's?

EXPLORE MORE

- Explore this reaction with trick birthday candles that won't go out. How long does it take before the birthday person simply gives up and laughs at the joke?

WHY IT MATTERS TO YOU

- When behaviors get a different and unpredictable response each time, it's like getting no response at all. If you receive little or no useful feedback about what is working and not working, what you are doing right or doing wrong, you end up feeling helpless...as if "things happen to me," not "I can make things happen." This is called *learned helplessness.*
- If you are ever in charge of training young people, remember how important it is to have the same rules all the time.
- Parents and children, husbands and wives, friends, coworkers, colleagues, and society as a whole...almost everyone can deal with almost anything if they only know what to expect.

DID YOU KNOW?

- Experiments have shown that babies who get their needs met when they cry don't become crybabies. Instead, they soon learn other, perhaps easier, ways to get their needs met. They also learn to do things for themselves and to have confidence in their own abilities to control the world around them.
- When animals are put in an unpleasant situation where there is no escape, they stop trying to escape. But when they are later put into another unpleasant situation where an easy escape is available, they still don't try to escape. Can you think of some behaviors this might help you to understand?
- Society usually makes one of two responses to people who have learned to be helpless. One response is to blame the people themselves ("They're lazy and getting what they deserve"). The other response is to "help" the people by giving them money. What helpless people really need is to learn that their actions can and do have results that can be predicted ahead of time. They need to experience how they control what happens to them.

THE TALLER ONE WINS	THE ONE WITH LONGER HAIR WINS	THE ONE WHOSE HOUSE IS CLOSER TO THE SCHOOL WINS	THE THINNER ONE WINS
THE SHORTER ONE WINS	THE ONE WITH SHORTER HAIR WINS	THE ONE WHOSE HOUSE IS FARTHER FROM THE SCHOOL WINS	THE HEAVIER ONE WINS
THE LIGHTER ONE WINS	THE ONE WITH STRAIGHTER HAIR WINS	THE ONE WITH MORE PETS WINS	THE ONE WEARING MORE RED WINS
THE DARKER ONE WINS	THE ONE WITH CURLIER HAIR WINS	THE ONE WITH FEWER PETS WINS	THE ONE WEARING MORE BLUE WINS

HOW WILL IT ALL TURN OUT?

The Most Important Experiment of All

Life has been compared to a play, a circus, even to a bowl of cherries. But if you really stop to think about it, life seems most like a lot of very exciting experiments, all going on at the same time. Your life is an experiment, and so is mine. When our paths cross—such as while you are reading this book—we are part of the same experiment.

You don't have to be a scientist to observe all of the life experiments going on around you, but you will see a lot more and get a lot more out of what you see if you remember some of the rules of scientific observation you have learned in *Psychology for Kids II:*

- Try to guess what people's expectations or "life hypotheses" might be. Consider how their expectations have influenced their successes and their failures.
- Think about your own life hypotheses. What sorts of things do you expect of others, of yourself, of life?
- What is your "operational definition" of success? Of failure? How will you decide if you have failed or if you have simply learned one more thing that doesn't work...perhaps on the way toward learning something that does work?
- What happens when you add things like hard work, knowledge, and responsibility to your own life experiment?
- What happens when you add an encouraging word or an extra measure of understanding to someone else's life experiment?

The experiment we shared—this book—is at an end, but the results are not in yet. Your experiments in psychology have taught you some of the basic rules behind human behavior. You have become more aware of why people act the way they do. You are better prepared to predict how people might respond to what you do and say. All of this new knowledge will influence what you see, what you do, and how your own personal life experiment turns out.

The fact that no two people go through life making all of the same decisions or meeting all of the same challenges makes each life a creative masterpiece—your own unique experiment. Knowing more about other people is sure to have a positive influence on your results.

Ask Yourself...

Now that you have read *Psychology for Kids II* and done some of the experiments...

1. Are you a better observer?
2. Are you asking more questions, doing more wondering?
3. Do you find that you are taking control of situations more often and looking for different approaches when you don't like how things are going?
4. Have your views of other people in your life—parents, other adults, young children, peers, teachers—changed at all?
5. Has your basic view of human nature changed at all? Find out by taking the quiz, "Are You a Diver or a Wader?," on pages 1–2. You may have taken this quiz before. If so, take it again. Then compare your results to find out if doing the experiments in this book has made any difference. (In science, this is called a "pre-test" and a "post-test").
6. Do you have a better idea now of what a psychologist is than you did before? (Can you spell psychology correctly? Close your eyes and try!)
7. Do you want to learn more about people and psychology? If so, how will you start? Who can you ask? Where can you go? You might begin by using some of your own ideas and questions and trying out your own experiments. Use the Ideas for More Experiments chart on page 8 to brainstorm plans for new discoveries.

Bibliography

Bandler, Richard. *Using Your Brain for a Change.* Moab, UT: Real People Press, 1985.

Briggs, John. *Fire in the Crucible.* Los Angeles: Jeremy P. Tarcher, Inc., 1990.

Chance, Paul. "Your Child's Self-Esteem." *Parents.* January 1982, pages 54–59.

Coon, Dennis. *Introduction to Psychology: Exploration and Application.* St. Paul, MN: West Publishing Company, 1992.

Cytowic, Richard E. *The Man Who Tasted Shapes.* New York: G.P. Putnam's Sons, 1993.

Edwards, Betty. *Drawing on the Artist Within.* New York: Simon & Schuster, Inc., 1987.

Feltman, R.S. *Elements of Psychology.* New York: McGraw-Hill, 1992.

Gardner, Howard. *Creating Minds.* New York: Basic Books, HarperCollins Publishers, 1993.

Gerow, J.R. *Psychology: An Introduction.* 3rd edition. Glenview, IL: Scott Foresman, 1992.

Gregory, Richard L. *The Oxford Companion to the Mind.* Oxford: Oxford University Press, 1987.

Hall, Edward T. *The Hidden Dimension.* New York: Anchor Books, Doubleday, 1990.

Hunt, Morton. *The Story of Psychology.* New York: Doubleday, 1993.

Kohn, Alfie. *Punished by Rewards.* Boston: Houghton Mifflin Company, 1993.

"Males and Females and What You May Not Know about Them." *Changing Times.* September 1981, pages 35–42.

Pines, Maya. "Can a Rock Walk?" *Psychology Today.* November 1983, pages 44–54.

Plotnik, R. *Introduction to Psychology.* 3rd edition. Pacific Grove, CA: Brooks-Cole, 1993.

Sdorow, L. *Psychology.* 2nd edition. Dubuque, IA: Wm. C. Brown, 1993.

Shepard, Roger N. *Mind Sights; Original Visual Illusions, Ambiguities, and Other Anomalies.* New York: W.H. Freeman and Co., 1990.

Snyder, Mark. "Self-Fulfilling Stereotypes." *Psychology Today.* July 1982, pages 60–68.

Wade, C., and C. Tavris. *Psychology.* 3rd edition. New York: HarperCollins, 1993.

Warga, Claire. "You Are What You Think." *Psychology Today.* September 1988, pages 55–58.

Winner, Ellen. "Where Pelicans Kiss Seals." *Psychology Today.* August 1986, pages 24–35.

Index

About the Author

Jonni Kincher received her education in psychology at California State University, San Bernardino. She now lives in Oregon.

Her interest in psychology began when she was in third grade, but there were not many psychology books for young children to read "back then." She made psychology available to young people by designing special courses in academic psychology for third grade through high school. Since these were the first courses to attempt teaching children psychology as an academic course, she had to create her own materials.

Jonni began teaching "Psychology for Kids Playshops" in 1983. "Kids" from ages 8–17 have "played" and learned about the subject of psychology in the Playshops. The ideas and materials for her books were developed and tested in the Playshops.

Jonni is also the author of three other books for Free Spirit Publishing: *Dreams Can Help: A Journal Guide to Understanding Your Dreams and Making Them Work for You, The First Honest Book about Lies,* and the award-winning *Psychology for Kids: 40 Fun Tests That Help You Learn about Yourself.*

Other Great Books from Free Spirit

Psychology for Kids
40 Fun Tests That Help You Learn About Yourself
by Jonni Kincher
Based on sound psychological concepts, these fascinating tests promote self-discovery, self-awareness, and self-esteem and empower young people to make good choices. For ages 10 & up.
$14.95; 152 pp.; softcover; illus.; 8½" x 11"

The Kid's Guide to Service Projects
Over 500 Ideas for Young People Who Want to Make a Difference
by Barbara A. Lewis
This guide has something for everyone who wants to make a difference, from simple projects to large-scale commitments. Kids can choose from a variety of topics. For ages 10 & up.
$12.95; 184 pp.; softcover; 6" x 9"

Fighting Invisible Tigers
A Stress Management Guide for Teens
Revised & Updated
by Earl Hipp
Proven, practical advice for teens on coping with stress, being assertive, building relationships, taking risks, making decisions, dealing with fears, and more.
For ages 11 & up.
$12.95; 160 pp.; softcover; illus.; 6" x 9"

What Do You Stand For?
A Kid's Guide to Building Character
by Barbara A. Lewis
This book empowers children and teens to identify and build character traits. Inspiring quotations, activities, true stories, and resources make this book timely, comprehensive, and fun.
For ages 11 & up.
$19.95; 284 pp.; softcover; B&W photos and illus.; 8½" x 11"

A Leader's Guide to Fighting Invisible Tigers
12 Sessions on Stress Management and Lifeskills Development
by Connie C. Schmitz, Ph.D., with Earl Hipp
Twelve independent, flexible step-by-step sessions teach specific stress-management skills. For grades 6–12.
$19.95; 136 pp.; softcover; 8½" x 11"

Worth the Risk
True Stories About Risk Takers Plus How You Can Be One, Too
by Arlene Erlbach
In an era when risk taking is most often associated with dangerous behavior, this uplifting book points out the benefits of taking a chance. Includes 20 first-person stories about young risk takers. For ages 10–15.
$12.95; 136 pp.; softcover; B&W photos; 6" x 9"

Perfectionism
What's Bad About Being Too Good?
Revised and Updated Edition
by Miriam Adderholdt, Ph.D., and Jan Goldberg
This revised and updated edition includes new research and statistics on the causes and consequences of perfectionism, biographical sketches of famous perfectionists and risk takers, and resources for readers who want to know more. For ages 13 & up.
$12.95; 136 pp.; softcover; illus.; 6" x 9"

School Power
Strategies for Succeeding in School
by Jeanne Shay Schumm, Ph.D., and Marguerite C. Radencich, Ph.D.
This book for school success covers everything students need to know, including how to get organized, take notes, study smarter, write better, follow directions, handle homework, and more. For ages 11 & up.
$13.95; 132 pp.; softcover; B&W photos and illus.; 8½" x 11"

To place an order or to request a free catalog of SELF-HELP FOR KIDS® and SELF-HELP FOR TEENS® materials, please write, call, email, or visit our Web site:

Free Spirit Publishing Inc.
400 First Avenue North • Suite 616 • Minneapolis, MN 55401-1724
toll-free 800.735.7323 • local 612.338.2068 • fax 612.337.5050
help4kids@freespirit.com • www.freespirit.com